PRAISE FOR
FIRE ON THE HORIZON

Winkey Pratney is a man who embodies a relevant message that actually touches the hearts of young people. He imparts a deep sense of confidence along with practical instruction on how a young person can be used by the Holy Spirit. I encourage parents to read this book.

MIKE BICKLE
Ministry Director, Friends of the Bridegroom
Senior Pastor, Metro Christian Fellowship of Kansas City

Winkey Pratney has a prophetic grasp of the destiny of this generation. He shows how that which is despised and rejected by the world will be used mightily of God. This book sounds a wake-up call to the Church, calling us to a new level of purity and devotion and to embrace with an open heart the coming move of God. Christians everywhere should read this.

GARY D. BLACK
President, Rock the Nation
Colorado Springs, Colorad

Winkie Pratney has been a prophet in youth ministry for decades. He understands the twenty-first-century young person and the culture he must fight against to stay radically committed to Christ. Everyone in youth ministry must read this book.

JIM BURNS
President, National Institute of Youth Ministry
San Juan Capistrano, California

Winkie Pratney is a hero to thousands of us in many nations. His teachings interpret the kingdom of God for the youth culture like nobody else I know. Just a glance at the chapter headings and you know you're in for a wild ride through technology, the culture of modernity and the intervention of the Almighty.

JOHN DAWSON
Founder, International Reconciliation Coalition
Ventura, California

In an age of high-definition CDs, DVDs and TVs, God has given us Winkie Pratney. With a prophetic voice, he defines with precision what was, what is and what's coming. *Fire on the Horizon* is high-definition reading.

GREGG JOHNSON
President, Movement Makers International

In *Fire on the Horizon*, Winkie Pratney demonstrates his profound ability to summarize the past, analyze the present, and give a glimpse of what the future might hold for a new generation in revival. It provokes you to think, *Wow! I was born at an important time in history. What part am I to play in this global youth revival?*

RON LUCE
President, Teen Mania

Winkie Pratney's strategic book *Fire on the Horizon* is packed with hard-hitting relevant truth that challenges me to partner with the Holy Spirit during this world-changing era of human history. If you have the heart of a "kamikaze" or even *want* that kind of focused spiritual passion, *Fire on the Horizon* is must-reading for you. Just don't try to read it before bedtime—it will do everything *but* put you to sleep!

JEANNE MAYO
Cross Current Youth and Young Adult Outreach
Rockford, Illinois

The radical concepts that Winkie Pratney expresses in this book are new to this generation, primarily because the majority of us have never truly experienced the fire of God. This book will undoubtedly be a catalyst for igniting the fires of revival in the hearts of this generation of young people.

JOSEPH THOMPSON
Associate Pastor, New Life Church
Colorado Springs, Colorado

FIRE ON THE HORIZON

THE SHAPE OF A TWENTY-FIRST-CENTURY YOUTH AWAKENING

WINKIE PRATNEY

Renew
FROM GOSPEL LIGHT

A DIVISION OF GOSPEL LIGHT
VENTURA, CALIFORNIA, U.S.A.

Published by Renew Books
A Division of Gospel Light
Ventura, California, U.S.A.
Printed in U.S.A.

Renew Books is a ministry of Gospel Light, an evangelical Christian pub-
lisher dedicated to serving the local church. We believe God's vision for
Gospel Light is to provide church leaders with biblical, user-friendly materials that will help them evangelize, disciple and minister to children,
youth and families.

It is our prayer that this Renew book will help you discover biblical truth
for your own life and help you meet the needs of others. May God richly
bless you.

*For a free catalog of resources from Renew Books and Gospel Light please call your
Christian supplier, or contact us at 1-800-4-GOSPEL or at www.gospellight.com.*

All Scripture quotations, unless otherwise indicated, are taken from the *New
King James Version.* Copyright © 1979, 1980, 1982 by Thomas Nelson, Inc.
Publishers. Used by permission. All rights reserved. All emphasis within
Scripture quotations is the author's own.

Other version used is:
KJV—King James Version. Authorized King James Version.

Cover Design by Kevin Keller
Interior Design by Debi Thayer
Edited by David Webb

LIBRARY OF CONGRESS CATALOGING-IN-PUBLICATION DATA
Pratney, Winkie, 1944–
    Fire on the horizon : the shape of a twenty-first century youth awakening/
Winkie Pratney.
        p.   cm.
    ISBN 0-8307-2426-5 (trade paper)
    1. Youth—Religious life.   2. Christian life.   I. Title.
    BV4531.2.P696 1998   99-12030
    269—dc21   CIP

1 2 3 4 5 6 7 8 9 10 11 12 / 05 04 03 02 01 00 99

Rights for publishing this book in other languages are contracted by Gospel
Literature International (GLINT). GLINT also provides technical help for the
adaptation, translation and publishing of Bible study resources and books in
scores of languages worldwide. For further information, write to GLINT at
P.O. Box 4060, Ontario, CA 91761-1003, U.S.A. You may also send e-mail to
Glintint@aol.com, or visit their web site at www.glint.org.

All song lyrics used by permission.

CONTENTS

PROLOGUE

As a child, I was always fascinated with fire. From the first time I lit a match through my boyhood years of building and testing rocket engines in my lab and making our own fireworks displays for the neighborhood, fire was on my mind. Fire is on God's mind too. Five hundred and forty-nine times in five hundred and six different verses, God's Book, the Bible, speaks of fire.

Fire on the Horizon is a look at two kinds of divine fire: one the fire of God's judgement and the other the fire of His awakening. Cultures dealt with by God are always caught in a race between revival and impending judgement. Ours is a culture dealt with by God and fire—of one kind or the other, ready or not—is blazing its way toward us as you read this.

Part One of this book deals with irresistible forms of *judgement fire*—the things that still terrify us even in a self-sufficient, insulated, technologically competent civilization. These are the fires God reserves for getting the attention of a people who are not listening. Judgement fires appear more and more in our popular media where they can be just watched as movies and hopefully not faced as realities. But like it or not, the Church had better be prepared for a judgement hour. If it is not primarily meant for us, His judgement will still begin at the house of God, and the way we respond when He begins to deal with our nations is critical to the fulfillment of His purposes on the earth.

Part Two looks at the strangeness of our times, more particularly what is happening in the Church as we near the edge of the new Millennium. We don't want to repeat history, but if we do not see the future, we will have no choice but to live through lessons again we should already have learned.

Parts Three and Four are about the *fire of awakening*. This portion of the book is for those to whom the core of this book is

addressed—to the young of this hour, born into the most unusual time in Western history. As William Barclay said, "There has
never been a time when it has been more difficult to be a
Christian. And there has never been a time when it has been more
necessary." In these chapters, I trust young hearts will see that the
God of all time and space has not forgotten or forsaken them and
that, contrary to popular sociological opinion, their participa-
tion may be vital to the greatest demonstration of His divine
greatness and glory in all of human history.

Parents, you need to know two things about this current
revival: First, *it isn't for you*. It is crafted by Christ for your kids.
You, of course, can get in on it, because all the promises of God
are "yea" and "amen" in Christ Jesus (see 2 Corinthians 1:20). He
is no respecter of persons (see Romans 2:11, *KJV*) and His mercies
are new every morning (see Lamentations 3:22,23). You may be
drafted to help and encourage and even minister to them. But
this revival was not designed for you. You had your day, and now
it is their turn.

Second, the reason it is sometimes so weird is *because your kids
are weird*. In many ways your children are more different today
than any other generation in history—even yours. God knows
them profoundly, and He has crafted what He is doing to the
exact shape of their need and their calling. When you see what
they face and what they are like as a generation, the purposes of
God in doing what He has done will become, I trust, clear enough
for you to avoid all-too-easy criticism and to begin to thank Him
afresh for His unusual and ever-creative communication to children no one else can talk to and no one else can touch.

Kids, you need to know something about God that will help
you face the future: Believe it or not, you are *a very special generation*. You are not an accident or an afterthought in the purposes
of the Lord. You have been brought onto the stage of history at a
critical time, and He has a work for you that He has waited for
centuries to accomplish. This book will, I hope, help you to see

what He is doing in the world and what your part is in all this.

Some years ago, a Native American friend of mine, who was called by the Lord to minister to several tribes, was given a vision. He saw an Indian warrior silhouetted on a horse in the intense red glow of a massive sun low on the horizon. Shocked and more than a little afraid, he asked, "Lord, what does this mean? Is this the sunset of my people?"

"No," came the reply. "It is the sunrise."

God knows your name and has your number. What He has done and will yet do to get your attention may bother others but really *touch* you. What He is doing now is bringing in a wave of young people who never knew what He was like and revealing Himself in ways they never dreamed.

Fire on the Horizon is a book about a new day when the Son of Righteousness will arise for all the world to see His glory. And you, with God helping you, can get in on it. *Go for it.*

Your brother in Jesus —

Winkie Pratney
A.D. 1999

PART I

JUDGEMENT CALL: MILLENNIUM-EDGE DISASTER MOVIES

"I came to send fire on the earth, and how I wish it were already kindled!"

Luke 12:49

John answered, saying to all, "I indeed baptize you with water; but One mightier than I is coming, whose sandal strap I am not worthy to loose. He will baptize you with the Holy Spirit and fire. His winnowing fan is in His hand, and He will thoroughly clean out His threshing floor, and gather the wheat into His barn; but the chaff He will burn with unquenchable fire."

Luke 3:16,17

"Therefore as the tares are gathered and burned in the fire, so it will be at the end of this age."

Matthew 13:40

Ah, you may leave here, for four days in space,
But when you return, it's the same old place.
The poundin' of the drums, the pride and disgrace,
You can bury your dead, but don't leave a trace,
Hate your next-door neighbor,
but don't forget to say grace,
And you tell me over and over and over
again my friend,
Ah, you don't believe we're on the eve of destruction.

— Barry McGuire
"Eve of Destruction"
Lyrics by P. F. Sloan

It's the end of the world as we know it, and I feel fine.

— R.E.M.
"The End of the World as We Know It"

OUTBREAK IN THE HOT ZONE: DISEASE

We are stars now in the Dope Show.

— Marilyn Manson
"The Dope Show Mechanical Animals"

For the Lord thy God is a consuming
fire, even a jealous God.

Deuteronomy 4:24, *KJV*

"Therefore her plagues will come in one day—death
and mourning and famine. And she will be utterly
burned with fire, for strong is the
Lord God who judges her."

Revelation 18:8

Nations dealt with by God are always caught in a race between revival and impending judgement. In the toss-up of history, God has given us all two ends: One end we can think with and choose to surrender to Him; the other we can sit on and let "whatever" happen. Our future depends on which end we choose. Heads we win; tails we lose.

God has four distinct ways of gaining the attention of any

nation that no longer listens to the preaching of His Word or the speaking of His Spirit. With all our modern technology, we are utterly helpless to control our own destiny when met by these devices of the Pale Rider, the horseman of the apocalypse whose name is Death. They are disease, environmental disaster, economic judgement or famine, and war (see Revelation 6:8).

God will shut up the heavens, take His hand of protection off the land, even allow alien invasion to get our attention. He loves us too much to let us go to hell without a warning. Let's look at the first of His judgements: disease.

THE WHORE OF BABYLON AND THE DRUGGING OF AMERICA

> For we wrestle not against flesh and blood, but against principalities, against powers, against the rulers of the darkness of this world, against spiritual wickedness in high places (Ephesians 6:12, *KJV*).

A principality is not necessarily a person or spirit. A principality is often an entity formed originally for a designed end that takes on a life of its own—a power that retains its original purpose but tends to self-replicate even beyond the life of its mortal founders. The Ford Motor Company is a principality. Bank of America is a principality. Kodak, IBM, Microsoft, Heinz, Disney and Proctor & Gamble are all principalities.

Babylon is no longer here as a city. Babylon the city is gone, buried, washed away on the tides of divine time. Nebuchadnezzar's ancient empire will not rise again to threaten the cities of our day. Despite Saddam Hussein's sad dream of immortalization by putting his name with Nebuchadnezzar's on the bricks of his buildings and his face beside the one God Himself calls the gold head of all the world's kingdoms, the buildings of Babel will never again be the dominant talk of the time. Babylon the city, Babylon the kingdom, Babylon of old is over and out. Babylon, geophysically the greatest empire of all time, will never rise again. God said it Himself (see Isaiah 13:19,20).

> Because of the wrath of the Lord she shall not be inhabited, but she shall be wholly desolate. Everyone who goes by Babylon shall be horrified and hiss at all her plagues (Jeremiah 50:13).

Babylon the beautiful, wonder of the ancient world, crossed God and died. Yet as He draws aside the curtains at the end of time, there, in mystery, is that great city, still locked in mortal combat with the people of God, a Babylon alive with violence and power, full of lust and greed and murder and hatred. Babylon the great, Babylon the enemy of Christ. Babylon is a demonic principality.

> And another angel followed, saying, "Babylon is fallen, is fallen, that great city, because she has made all nations drink of the wine of the wrath of her fornication" (Revelation 14:8).

> And he cried mightily with a loud voice, saying, "Babylon the great is fallen, is fallen, and has become a dwelling place of demons, a prison for every foul spirit, and a cage for every unclean and hated bird!" (Revelation 18:2).

The book of Revelation depicts Babylon as a spiritual pattern, a counterfeit bride of Christ, a hooking, chaining, controlling structure now possessed with its own demonic existence and personality. Babylon is the *world's master spirit*, the principality that controls the age of the End.

And upon her forehead was a name written, MYSTERY, BABYLON THE GREAT, THE MOTHER OF HARLOTS AND ABOMINATIONS OF THE EARTH (Revelation 17:5, *KJV*).

No one says Babylon lacks class. Its world is filled with luxury, trade, travel, culture, music and art. It dresses like royalty (see Revelation 18:16), does its deals in precious metals and gems (see v. 12), demands nothing but the best of everything (see v. 14). Yet Babylon addicts, enslaves and imprisons. The ultimate end of its traffic is to *make slaves of the bodies and souls of men* (see v. 13). Its precincts are the homes of devils and the hideouts of filthy spirits, its spawn immorality, violence, sin—everything God hates most.

Babylon the merciless, occultic hater that preys on both the young and the old, Babylon hungering to live and rule forever in order to play God *has an appointment with justice.*

Then a mighty angel took up a stone like a great millstone and threw it into the sea, saying, "Thus with violence the great city Babylon shall be thrown down, and shall not be found anymore. The sound of harpists, musicians, flutists, and trumpeters shall not be heard in you anymore. No craftsman of any craft shall be found in you anymore, and the sound of a millstone shall not be heard in you anymore. The light of a lamp shall not shine in you anymore, and the voice of bridegroom and bride shall not be heard in you anymore. *For your merchants were the great men of the earth, for by your sorcery all the nations were deceived"* (Revelation 18:21-23).

So what is the phenomenal, pervasive power with which Babylon holds sway over the bodies and souls of men and women, young and old? Well, what is the most lucrative business on earth? If you said real estate, aerospace, computers, software, entertainment, food, housing, sports or almost anything else listed in the annual reports of the Fortune 500 companies, you're probably wrong. What earns more *money* than any other industry on earth?

According to Scripture the power of Babylon is *pharmakia*, the word translated "sorceries" or "witchcraft," the thing that gives this principality its world power.[1] It is that which people have used from the first roots of rebellion as a substitute for the power and wisdom and provision of the living God. It is the word from which we derive the words "pharmacy" and "pharmaceutical." What is the great economy at the end of the world? The one we have now: The power of Babylon is *drugs*.

Notice I did not say *illegal* drugs. "Illegal" simply means *presently unauthorized by government*. Legal *pharmakia* alone is the biggest industry on earth, a multitrillion-dollar business unlike any other in human history. The wealthiest man on earth is probably not the astute Bill Gates, nor is it likely to be some Arab oil baron building an empire on the dwindling barreled remains of a dead world. Drug manufacturers routinely show profits *from 10,000 to 20,000 percent* on their products.

When the diet drug Phen-Fen was withdrawn from the market after a seven-year testing program required for FDA certification, it had earned for one company alone in that brief time more than *one billion dollars*. Olestra, Viagra, the list goes on. Chemotherapy for cancer alone is a trillion-dollar industry.

AIDS, EBOLA AND THE COMING PLAGUES OF THE TWENTY-FIRST CENTURY

America is in trouble. And so is the world she supplies.

Despite the best efforts of researchers and the pharmaceutical industry, death by infectious disease is rising. In the past fifteen years, it has climbed the charts from the number-five killer in the United States to number three with a bullet, closing in on cancer and heart disease. Ten years ago, it was impossible to find one case of drug-resistant pneumonia in America; in 1995, up to 25 percent of all adult pneumonia resisted treatment with penicillin. Specific states reported even higher resistance—from 30 to 60 percent!

Some strains resist multiple-drug treatment. Many experts fear a return to the 1940s when pneumonia was one of the most common causes of death. Viruses and bacteria are "learning" to share with other strains immunity acquired on a DNA level by a process of plasma exchange on a microbiotic level, creating new and deadly forms of infectious agents utterly immune to previous treatments.

In the '70s a shot of penicillin was all it took to cure gonorrhea. Today in places like Hong Kong, penicillin is useless against 77.9 percent of gonorrhea cases; in the Philippines *all* strains of gonorrhea are drug resistant. In New York a full *third* of all cases of tuberculosis (TB) are caused by bacteria that resist antibiotics. It doesn't take much to get TB going; just a cough or sneeze, a conversation up close and the germ is in the air. If you are infected with one of the drug-resistant strains of TB, you have about a 70 percent chance of survival. Those are the same odds you would have had *before* antibiotics were invented!

Then there are the "glamorous" killers, the incurable headline-grabbers like AIDS, Ebola Zaire and the hantavirus. We are again sitting on the verge of an outbreak of plague of biblical proportions.

> A hot virus in extreme amplification can fill an eye-dropper of blood with 100 million particles. The host is possessed by a life-form attempting to convert the host into itself . . . a molecular shark, a motive without mind, hard, logical and totally selfish (Richard Preston, *The Hot Zone*, p. 19).

The Centers for Disease Control in Atlanta is begging researchers to find new antibiotics—but this will only postpone the plague. These bugs are smart and skilled. They adapt to resist all man-made drugs, and they come back stronger and deadlier than before.

Antibiotics are credited with having saved millions of lives, but for the past thirty years doctors have handed them out like lollipops. Now these powerful drugs are *breeding* disease. They kill without discrimination, taking out the "friendly" bacteria as well as the bad, thus creating in us an unnatural, unstable condition in which we are defenseless against invasion by new mutant strains of disease that kill so quickly there's no medical way to fight them.[2]

By the very nature of this judgement, heightened drug use is increasingly powerless to halt or reverse disease. Since we can hardly expect to defeat any enemy we serve, we need believers who will not bow to the spirit of sorcery and not accept this force revealed in Scripture as a substitute for the power of God and the principles of God's Word in dealing with disease.

George Fox, founder of the Quakers and supernatural radical of the 1700s, said that God gave him insight into three worlds which had deeply departed from God's original purposes: the world of theology, the world of law and the world of medicine. John Wesley wrote a book on home health remedies (*Primitive Medicine*) that was in use for more than a century, and he even experimented with his own early electrical machine as an aid to promote healing.

It is time we begin to see our bodies as temples of the Holy Spirit, subject to His laws that cannot be violated without consequence. While we can thank Him for Christian doctors who have given their talents to Him, we cannot continue to plead for Him to shore up our enemy-infested immune systems by divine intervention while trying unsuccessfully to serve two masters. We must return to biblical ways of dealing with disease, seek God for genuine answers to health issues and stop looking to *pharmakia* as our automatic answer to pain, disease and suffering.[3]

NOTES

1. Every biblical mention of drugs is in a context of despair, mourning, grief and danger. They are never connected with healing. *Pharmakia* "primarily signifies the use of medicine, drugs, spells; then poisoning; then sorcery, witchcraft" (*Vine's Expository Dictionary*, NT Words) or "medication, by extension magic" (*Strong's*, #533). The word is used to indicate one of the four sins men do not repent of at the end of time in Revelation 9:21 (the others are theft, fornication and murder). Prescribed medical drugs alone are so toxic they kill 130,000 Americans every year (*Johns Hopkins Medical Letter*).
2. The polio vaccine may have conquered polio strains 1, 2 and 3, but we've since identified 69 more strains. Some cripple, some kill, some merely cause flu-like symptoms and then remain in your body for years to reemerge 20 or 30 years later in the form of a mysterious Chronic Fatigue or the Epstein-Barr/Guillain-Barr syndrome, for which there is no known cure. Salk oral polio vaccine was cultivated from the pus of dead-pig kidneys and given to every child in the U.S. Retested in the 1970s, it was found to contain more than 147 live strains of other forms of polio and has since been taken off the market. Crib death, autism, dyslexia, attention deficit disorder: all "mysterious illnesses" of the twentieth century? Not according to researchers in Europe, Asia and Australia; scientists worldwide have already admitted that the DPT vaccine is a likely cause of asthma and crib death (a.k.a. sudden infant death syndrome). Many researchers warn if the mass-vaccination programs continue as they are—routinely mangling our immune systems and causing the appearance of mutant viruses—we are in for an infection holocaust. A growing body of evidence suggests that childhood diseases (most of which are relatively harmless) are critical stepping stones to developing a strong, fully-functioning immune system. Vaccines which rob your body of its ability to practice on minor illnesses may well stunt your immune system. Since the MMR (measles, mumps, rubella) vaccine was marketed and mandated for every child in the U. S., the average age of kids contracting these diseases moved from ages 5-9 to ages 10 and older, only shifting the onset of measles to an age at which it is more dangerous (*Health Science Institute Report*, summer 1997).
3. See appendix for the recipe for making and using Master Tonic, a *natural* antibiotic.

ARMAGEDDON:
HELL FROM THE HEAVENS

Dear Lord, I sincerely hope you're coming
'Cause you really started something.

— Elvis Costello
"Waiting for the End of the World"

Something strange is happening to the weather across the world. We can look at past weather patterns, chart the movement of El Niño, measure the hole in the ozone layer and postulate theories based on global warming and changing levels of carbon dioxide in the atmosphere, but in the final analysis we can do nothing but watch. We are wholly at the mercy of the heavens.

SOLAR FLARES, HEAT WAVES AND THE WEIRDING OF THE WEATHER

Only three times in biblical history did God stop the predictable sight of the sun in the sky. The first time He delayed a day so an army could win (see Joshua 10:12-14). The second time He turned back the clock of the heavens to show a faithful man His willingness to listen to his prayer (see 2 Kings 20:8-11). And the last time He was here Himself, dying for the sins of the world (see Luke 23:45).

Yet we are warned there is a day coming when the sun will not be darkened, but the very heavens will catch fire on that day. A terrible flare has been reserved for the end of this planet, and all that is on Earth will be burned (see Revelation 20:9). A hundred years ago, this biblical warning was scoffed at by the scientific elite of the day. "Where would you get a fire big enough to burn a whole world?" they laughed.

Nobody scoffs anymore. We instead make blockbuster movies about threats from above—movies that hold out hope that our best and brightest, armed with the latest technology, will brave the hostile heavens and save the world. *But we still look at the sky and sometimes feel afraid.*

> But the heavens and the earth which are now preserved by the same word, are reserved for fire until the day of judgment and perdition of ungodly men (2 Peter 3:7).

> Looking for and hastening the coming of the day of God, because of which the heavens will be dissolved, being on fire, and the elements will melt with fervent heat (2 Peter 3:12).

The thing that finally got to Pharaoh was the hail and the fire. He never said he sinned before the heavens over his head became hostile. Sometimes it takes something in the sky to get our attention, to show us our true condition. Arrogant to the last, Pharaoh never had a chance. The Lord hardened his heart, locked him into the judgement he had treasured up over the years, and no false confession and surface repentance was going to get him out of it this time. From the moment the command went out from God, the very air over Egypt was charged with menace; from this time on, darkness, locusts and finally death would come selectively to all the land.

> Then the Lord said to Moses, "Stretch out your hand toward heaven, that there may be hail in all the land of

Egypt—on man, on beast, and on every herb of the field, throughout the land of Egypt."

And Moses stretched out his rod toward heaven; and the Lord sent thunder and hail, and fire darted to the ground. And the Lord rained hail on the land of Egypt. So there was hail, and fire mingled with the hail, so very heavy that there was none like it in all the land of Egypt since it became a nation. And the hail struck throughout the whole land of Egypt, all that was in the field, both man and beast; and the hail struck every herb of the field and broke every tree of the field. Only in the land of Goshen, where the children of Israel were, there was no hail.

And Pharaoh sent and called for Moses and Aaron, and said to them, "I have sinned this time. The Lord is righteous, and my people and I are wicked" (Exodus 9:22-27).

Second Chronicles 7:13,14 deals with not only the forgiveness of the people but also the healing of the land. There is no known technology that can save us from the heavens of brass. *The only way we can affect the weather is, in the mercy of God, heartfelt repentance, humility and prayer.*

It is a little-explored fact that in both Scripture and history God has spoken to nations through the weirding of the weather. The Fall in the garden affected not only mankind, but it also affected the entire creation linked to him by the fiat of God. Nature is one of those few areas left affecting the life of technological man in which he remains basically helpless, where all his schemes and plans and dreams lie utterly powerless before the irresistible fury of the very elements around him, when self-reliance fails and all that is left is prayer and a hope for divine intervention of mercy.

What will you do when the wind or the water comes, when the ground shakes like a sea or the sky turns to molten lead and everything around you starts to die? Atheists are rare during the weirding of the weather.

> And a great windstorm arose, and the waves beat into the boat, so that it was already filling. But [Jesus] was in the stern, asleep on a pillow. And they awoke Him and said to Him, "Teacher, do You not care that we are perishing?"
>
> Then He arose and rebuked the wind, and said to the sea, "Peace, be still!" And the wind ceased and there was a great calm. But He said to them, "Why are you so fearful? How is it that you have no faith?"
>
> And they feared exceedingly, and said to one another, "Who can this be, that even the wind and the sea obey Him!" (Mark 4:37-41).

Jesus rebuked the storm. The disciples who were deeply afraid of the storm before were terrified beyond measure when with a single order Christ stopped the raging wind. "Quiet!" He commanded, speaking to the wind and the weather as if it were a snarling dog, and the storm backed off, instantly cowed. ("Sorry! Didn't know You were in the boat.")

Not all storms are sent by God, just as the Lord is not always in the fire, the wind or the earthquake. But after the fire, the wind and the quake, there is the "still small voice" (1 Kings 19:12). When the weather has our attention, when the sky or the ground or the sea are finished talking terror, we may be ready to listen.

When the Pilgrims first came to America, they experienced an unseasonably dry, hot summer—no rain for almost three months. Their meager crops began to die, and the Indians who watched them knew these people were going to die too. But the Pilgrims knew something about the relationship of weather to the dealings of God with men. They understood the spiritual link between our morals and the creation around us.

Setting aside a solemn day for prayer, fasting and repentance, they asked God's mercy. Although it was a hot, cloudless sky morning and afternoon, near evening clouds began to gather and sweet, gentle showers began to fall. The rain so thoroughly soaked the parched ground that the crops were wonderfully revived—to the astonishment of the Indians, who knew it was not nature but nature's God. Governor William Bradford's 1647 account says "for which mercy . . . they set aside a day of Thanksgiving." Such weather interventions in history show the deep correlation of prayer, repentance and child-like trust with the divine healing of the land, or the weather.[1]

> No more let sins and sorrows grow
> Nor thorns infest the ground,
> He comes to make the blessings flow
> Far as the curse is found.

> — Isaac Watts, "Joy to the World"

NOTE

1. A similar incident took place a century later in Charles Finney's day. "The summer of 1853 was unusually hot and dry; pastures were scorched. There seemed likely to be a total crop failure. At the church in Oberlin the great congregation had gathered as usual. Though the sky was clear, the burden of Finney's prayer was for rain: 'We do not presume, Oh Lord, to dictate to Thee what is best for us; yet Thou didst invite us to come to Thee as children to an earthly Father and tell Thee all our wants. We want rain. Our pastures are dry. The earth is gaping open for rain. The cows are wandering about and lowing in search of water. Even the squirrels are suffering from thirst. Unless Thou givest us rain our cattle will die and our harvest will come to naught. Oh Lord, send us rain and send it now! This is an easy thing for Thee to do. Send it now Lord, for Christ's sake.' In a few minutes he had to cease preaching; his voice could not be heard because of the roar and rattle of the rain!" (*Life of Finney: Springs in the Valley*, Mrs. Chas. Cowman, pp. 251, 252).

THE DAY OF THE LOCUST: ECOLOGICAL DISASTER

A fire devours before them, and behind them a flame
burns; the land is like the Garden of Eden before
them, and behind them a desolate wilderness; surely
nothing shall escape them.

Joel 2:3

A locust swarm in the Middle East may be two or three miles wide, up to twenty miles long and so thick that when they fly over a doomed land they blot out the sun. What the first wave of millions misses, the larvae they leave behind will kill later. In 1988, one swarm of billions rode a hurricane from Africa to the Caribbean. If that swarm had hit Central Park in New York, in one day not a single tree or blade of grass would have been left alive.

Nothing we know short of divine intervention can stop a swarm. When God wanted to show Joel the reality of judgement and revival, He showed him an army of locusts coming to his land. What can be done when even nature is against us?

THE "BEASTS OF THE FIELD" MULTIPLY AGAINST US

The most dangerous predator of man in the world other than man himself is, strangely enough, the *mosquito*. Diseases spread through this one-millimeter vampire kill hundreds of thousands of humans annually. We prepare and think big when it comes to dealing with possible threats to our very existence, but it is often the little things that take us out unexpectedly.

Herod was eaten up by worms and died when, in his pompous oration, he gave the impression that he was no longer human, but a god (see Acts 12:20-23). A mere medfly took a governor out of office in California. If men of God split atoms instead of theological or cultural hairs, they would realize that the power of God is most often latent in little things. When judgement comes to a land, you must watch out for even the dust of the ground.

God put a fear in the animals when man, the given keeper of the garden, started killing for pleasure. We still wantonly abuse this connected creation, choosing to believe they have no say in the matter. But God is a God of justice, and the animate creation has a life and purpose of its own before the Lord. He will not suffer abuse to go unspoken and unchecked.

If we insist on destroying what God has given us, what we take so much for granted will turn on us. The beasts of the field will multiply against us, the birds will be messengers of judgement, the frogs and the flies will preach to our hardened hearts. Technology cannot save us on that day; only true and contrite repentance will do. The healing of the land is the last part of the promise of revival.

But when Paul had gathered a bundle of sticks and laid them on the fire, a viper came out because of the heat, and fastened on his hand. But he shook off the creature into the fire and suffered no harm (Acts 28:3,5).

Sometimes when you go out into the world to speak about Christ, snakes will come out of the fire. The lighting of the flame reveals the hidden viper in the wood, and it comes out fighting, hurting and biting. People watching may jump to the conclusion that such a blatant attack is a judgement of God on your arrival, but if they see that the bites do not cause you any harm, they may make the opposite mistake and believe you are a god. Missionaries are neither to be unwelcome nor worshiped. We are neither enemies nor deities; we are simply God's servants. Yet wherever the gospel goes, you can expect snakes and healing.

God never promised supernatural ministry in a supportive environment. Mission fields are messy and dangerous, but people and places that are already whole don't need healing.

> I said, "Let me walk in the field."
> He said, "No, walk in the town."
> I said, "But there are no flowers there."
> He said, "No flowers, but a crown."
> I said, "But the sky is black—
> There is nothing but noise and din."
> But He wept as He sent me back.
> "There is more," He said. "There is sin."
>
> — Author Unknown

Elijah not only called down a day of destruction on the land; *he lived in it himself.* The prophet often must share in the consequences of his prophecy in order for him to feel the hurt God feels when He must bring judgement upon a nation. Christians will not always escape what happens, but they need not feel their suffering is due to personal sin.

"Get away from here and turn eastward, and hide by the Brook Cherith, which flows into the Jordan. And it will be that you shall drink from the brook, and I have commanded the ravens to feed you there."

So he went and did according to the word of the Lord, for he went and stayed by the Brook Cherith, which flows into the Jordan. The ravens brought him bread and meat in the morning, and bread and meat in the evening; and he drank from the brook.

And it happened after a while that the brook dried up, because there had been no rain in the land (1 Kings 17:3-7).

Even in the midst of terrible famine, God set His man by a brook that still ran and sent him food each day via natural airmail.

Yet one day the brook dried up. If it had not dried up, he might have gained an arrogance, lost his compassion and begun to look to the brook and the birds for his provision instead of the One who provided them. Instead, he is moved to a place where a widow woman is about to eat her last meal with her son and then die. In the providence of God, a woman and her child can reveal much more of God than a brook and the birds (see 1 Kings 17:8-16).

In times of divine disaster, we are called not just to survive ourselves but to minister to and serve others who have no idea at all why there is no rain for so long.

TITANIC AND Y2K: ECONOMIC MELTDOWN

Q. What do you get when you cross the Atlantic with the *Titanic*?
A. Halfway.

Q. What do you get when you try to cross God?
A. Nothing, man. Nothing at all.

The luxury ocean liner *Titanic* was a living parable of its time—the ultimate product of the Industrial Age, a mammoth tribute to technology, wealth and power that single-handedly stood for all that was deemed wonderful in a world that had largely written God off as an unnecessary factor in the equation of success. "Mister," one observer was heard to say, "God himself couldn't sink this ship."[1]

It doesn't take much imagination or insight to trace the ensuing disaster to human arrogance: Who needed a lot of lifeboats when God Himself couldn't sink the ship? White Star Line officials prodded the captain to push the engines on her maiden voyage to prove to the watching world just how awesome their accomplishment truly was.

The *Titanic* died at the icy hand of the very substance it moved in, killed by mere water turned to a finger of cold that cut through its hull like a surgical knife. On that "night to remember," this proud wonder of the world died in the cold of an empty sea. And on its swiftly tilting deck, the band at the last played "Nearer My God to Thee."[2]

Of course, *Titanic* is now only a movie with subplots of riches, romance and courage and chart-busting songs about love going on forever and hearts having minds of their own. And this is no longer the Industrial Age when men worshiped fire and steel and oil and the world revolved around the dreams wrought by pyrotechnology. This is the Information Age, when men instead worship the power of digital domain, of connection, network and communication. Yet a sea to conquer is there just the same, the boast of a new boat is still made. And again the cold illusion of an unsinkable dominion outside of God's rule will draw exactly the same judgement.

> Each one's work will become clear; for the Day will declare it, because it will be revealed by fire; and the fire will test each one's work, of what sort it is (1 Corinthians 3:13).

> That the genuineness of your faith, being much more precious than gold that perishes, though it is tested by fire, may be found to praise, honor, and glory at the revelation of Jesus Christ (1 Peter 1:7).

> Your gold and silver are corroded, and their corrosion will be a witness against you and will eat your flesh like fire. You have heaped up treasure in the last days (James 5:3).

We have looked to paper gold for what only God can properly provide. Jesus spoke at length about money and about *true* treasure. When He contrasted worship of the real God with idolatry,

He mentioned only one competing deity by name: Mammon, god of money (see Luke 16:13). An idol is a controllable representation of our dearest dreams and most significant focus. If we worship an imaginary God, we will have to put up with an imaginary salvation.

WHY 2K?

With the world increasingly connected on-line and the coin of our modern realm rooted in communication and information, no one could conceive as a prelude to disaster something as silly as the saving of two mere bytes of memory. Yet this is exactly what happened, and by the time pundits in 1995 saw the extent of the potential damage, it was far too late to reverse the tide of the coming technological *tsunami*.

With the division of labor splitting modern manufacturing into a multitude of interdependent suppliers, no company can even make a simple pencil today on its own. With power grids, water and food supplies and the financial records of nations almost wholly run by dumb digits that cannot distinguish between a new century and one that sprang into existence a hundred years ago, the Y2K bug is at once the silliest mistake and possibly the most disastrous threat to connected civilization ever. Simply put, *2K* is *Two Kingdoms* in conflict—the kingdom of Mammon versus the kingdom of God—and only those who have invested beyond earthly access will keep it all.

How Christians react to the chaos that comes to any country under judgement is always more important than what they can prepare for. The problem with unavoidable disaster is that given the nature of its purpose *it cannot really be escaped*. Knowing this, how must the child of God then react?

"But when you hear of wars and commotions, do not be terrified; for these things must come to pass first, but the end will not come immediately."

Then He said to them, "Nation will rise against nation, and kingdom against kingdom. And there will be great earthquakes in various places, and famines and pestilences; and there will be fearful sights and great signs from heaven.

"But before all these things, they will lay their hands on you and persecute you, delivering you up to the synagogues and prisons. You will be brought before kings and rulers for My name's sake. But *it will turn out for you as an occasion for testimony*" (Luke 21:9-13).

Wisdom dictates that we prepare within our power for what we know will come. Jesus' parable of the five wise and five foolish virgins (see Matthew 25:1-13) tells us that failure to see what *might* come means sometimes missing out even after being faithful in everything else.[3] But your reaction to uncontrollable disaster speaks volumes of the real state of your heart.

In what finally is your trust? The rich young ruler came with the right question to the right Person who had the right answer, but he went away in sorrow. Finally empty, he subsequently vanished from significant history. Peter we know, Thomas we know, even James the Less we know. Today in the twentieth century we don't even know this young man's name. Jesus did not chase him. The wind filled the sails of the boat in which Christ came, and He moved on while the world stood still forever around the man who might have been a follower of the One who owns it all.

Materialism is the hidden enemy of trust, the one thing that brings a cloud to the soul and blindness to the inner eyes with which we see the purposes of God. Little children, keep yourselves from idols.

NOTES

1. The *Titanic* cost $7.5 million to build, roughly $600 million in today's currency. A top first-class ticket went for $3,100, or the equivalent of $124,000 today, while a third-class ticket was $32 in 1912, approximately $1,300 today. The *Titanic* was the biggest, the most beautiful, the most technologically advanced and luxurious liner built up to that time. An unsinkable ship. The oddest thing about the *Titanic* disaster is that there was only one way she could sink—exactly the way she did—and the chances of that happening were infinitesimal. (Paula Parisi, *Titanic and the Making of James Cameron*, Newmarket Press, NY, 1998, p. 54.)

2. The lifeboats had a capacity of 1,178, barely half the number of the voyagers (1,320 passengers and 915 crew) that fateful night. Only 750 were rescued; the rest died. Many of them froze to death in the glacial North Atlantic waters. Most went down with her 46,378 tons of metal. The last trace of her disappeared at 2:20 A.M., only two hours and forty minutes after the collision (Parisi, p. 56).

3. Suggested preparation for economic, environmentally induced or invasion-produced disasters includes stockpiling key items like pure water, dried foods, auxiliary power sources like wind or solar generators, gas and oil reserves; turning stocks and paper securities into real-value metals like silver, gold and platinum; preparing to barter in the absence of cash; obtaining complete hard copies of all key documents like birth certificates, passports, bank records and policies. Armed survivalists are even preparing for life in hidden hill fortresses. Believers must do what they believe God has told them to do on the eve of disaster, but each strength carries its own built-in weakness. We can prepare for sharing in a nation under judgement, but the bottom line must always be commitment to the commands of God: Love Him and put Him first, and love your neighbor as you love yourself.

SAVING PRIVATE RYAN: GLOBAL WAR

For the eyes of the Lord run to and fro throughout the
whole earth, to show Himself strong on behalf of those
whose heart is loyal to Him. In this you have done
foolishly; therefore from now on you shall have wars.

2 Chronicles 16:9

"I will kindle a fire in the wall of Rabbah, and it
shall devour its palaces, amid shouting in the day of
battle, and a tempest in the day of the whirlwind.
I will send a fire upon Moab, and it shall devour the
palaces of Kerioth; Moab shall die with tumult, with
shouting and trumpet sound.
I will send a fire upon Judah, and it shall devour the
palaces of Jerusalem."

Amos 1:14; 2:2,5

War is a major theme of the Bible. I don't mind telling you it has
always bothered me that for a supposed book of a people of peace
there should be so many records of fighting in the Scriptures. If
the Israelites were not fighting the Amalekites, Philistines or
Canaanites, they were fighting each other. It was some years
before I understood one of the key reasons why these battles were
big deals in the Bible: *The world is at war with God.*

As C. S. Lewis said, God's creation is presently "enemy-occupied territory." The Church was never designed to function in a fallen world as a big party to which only the elect are invited. The Church was fashioned to be an army—born to fight and called to fight. When the members of the Church fight amongst themselves, the problem is not our attitude but our vision. We are *meant* to be warriors, and we're supposed to be *trained* to fight. But if we cannot see the real battle, the real enemy, we will turn and fight each other.

ESTABLISHING A BEACHHEAD

In the opening minutes of *Saving Private Ryan* (courtesy of Spielberg, Hanks and Co.) we see the terrible cost of establishing a beachhead. A beachhead is a place of strategic importance to the enemy. Though it's usually not the location of the bulk of the enemy occupational forces, it may be a key access point, a gateway to the soft underbelly of the invader. Beachheads are highly defended, and an attack on a beachhead is often costly. Only a few of the attacking forces may actually break through the lines of defense, but if they will hold the ground they have captured, they open the door for many others to pour through.

George Otis, Jr., in his book *Informed Intercession*, writes about the significance of spiritual beachheads. The enemy has his key pressure points, choking the arteries of our towns and cities and nations, and once they are found and identified then the *real* battle can begin.

Revival is a divine attack on society. When no one stands up for God, when He sees there is no one to stand in the gap and wonders that there is no intercessor, He puts on righteousness as a breastplate and the Son of God goes to war. The armor of God in Ephesians is not called this just because it is the armor God gives to His soldiers; it is also the armor He Himself puts on when it is time to take back what is rightfully His.

FIELD OF DREAMS

> Then Jeremiah said to Zedekiah, "Thus says the Lord, the God of hosts, the God of Israel: 'If you surely surrender to the king of Babylon's princes, then your soul shall live; this city shall not be burned with fire, and you and your house shall live.
>
> 'But if you do not surrender to the king of Babylon's princes, then this city shall be given into the hand of the Chaldeans; they shall burn it with fire, and you shall not escape from their hand'" (Jeremiah 38:17,18).

It is the business of prophets to see things kings cannot know and to speak things kings cannot bear. It is a hard thing to spend most of your young life telling those who don't want to listen what will happen if they don't. It is an even harder thing to see the fulfillment of your words from prison while the army of the enemy overruns your nation. It is the hardest thing of all to speak in the midst of hell new words of hope from heaven. But that is what prophets must do.

Jeremiah had been tossed into prison by Zedekiah, the king of Judah, for daring to prophesy that Jerusalem would be given into the hands of their enemies. And, as advertised, the armies of Babylon attacked the city. Meanwhile, the Lord spoke to Jeremiah, telling him his cousin Hanamel would visit him in prison with an offer to sell Jeremiah a piece of land in the middle of the war zone. And the Lord said he was to buy it! Now real estate—especially a piece of land under siege—was probably the last thing on Jeremiah's mind at this time, but as a matter of inheritance it was his right and responsibility to purchase and possess this land. So when Hanamel came to him as promised, Jeremiah made the deal and pronounced it a sign to all present:

> For thus says the Lord of hosts, the God of Israel: "Houses and fields and vineyards shall be possessed again in this land" (Jeremiah 32:15).

The prophet who spent most of his young life in prison for telling the truth had seen the exact fulfillment of what God said to him happen before his eyes. With the enemy at the very gates of the city, in what is possibly the greatest example of faith outside of Abraham and Moses in the Old Testament, God instructed him to buy a field for the future.

The judgements of God are never simply punitive; God's purpose is always redemption, and even in the midst of judgement He still remembers mercy.

A GOVERNMENT BY THE PEOPLE, FOR THE PEOPLE

Much evangelical prayer went into the elections that opened the final decade before the New Millennium. The Church even ran candidates who professed Christ and gave testimony to their desire for righteous judgement. Yet to the chagrin of many, and despite the rallying around the polls of many purposeful Protestants, the nation's choice was another.

This was old news to one prophet who in a prophetic dream was given the banner headlines in five cities the day before the election. In the aftermath, naturally enough, some asked, "Why did we get a president like this one?"

The answer: "God said He was giving us a president who is better than we deserve."[1]

What we experienced a few years later was not just the exposure of a president's secret sins; it was the exposure of a nation. It has been a long, long time since a man who heads such corridors of power said to a watching nation, "I have sinned." Not since the days of David has there been such a confession.

It is a hard thing to know that God will use a king who is alien to His worship when His *own* people become alien to Him and irreverent in *their* worship. "The king's heart is in the hand of the Lord, like the rivers of water; He turns it wherever He wishes" (Proverbs 21:1). God calls world rulers like Nebuchadnezzar and Cyrus His servants and uses them as the heads of armies to bring judgement upon His own people for their departure from truth and justice. God is not a mere politician, but He does indeed give a nation the kind of government it deserves.

TERRITORIALISM

Item: Owing to its harsh abortion policies, China has some 100 million young men with no prospect of wife or job other than to serve in the present standing army—the largest in the world—which at present has nothing to do but to train for war. Reportedly, a great deal of Western start-up money going to launch new industries in China may be channeled instead to this military juggernaut, and some new Chinese maps show the nations surrounding the country as uniformly red—treated already as Chinese territory. Somebody is not saying something here.

War is a simple equation: You have it. I don't. I want it. I'll take it. Scripture asks, *Where do wars come from?* and answers directly,

From our own lusts (see James 4:1). It is a sign of the foolishness and greed of the last days that there will be wars, rumors of wars, and nation shall rise against nation.

TERRORISM

Item: There are purportedly at least two Middle Eastern universities (funded to the tune of more than a billion dollars per year from Arab oil) where young Islamic fundamentalists are trained in the core elements of a modern evangelist for the Party of God and the cause of Allah. They are taught Islamic law and doctrine, proper control of lifestyle and behavior and, of course, the usual studies in explosives, assassination and terrorism.

Who needs nuclear warheads when a passage to Paradise is guaranteed by a self-sacrificial act against the enemy in a Holy War? A few pounds of C4 strapped to a body, nerve gas stashed in a van, or even an engineered virus dropped into the water supply of a target nation can strike a blow for religious commitment in force and coercion of conscience. Wars today do not need large armies; only truly devoted soldiers.

HOW TO FACE A DEN OF LIONS

You shall tread upon the lion and the cobra, the young lion and the serpent you shall trample underfoot.

"Because he has set his love upon Me, therefore I will deliver him; I will set him on high, because he has known My name. He shall call upon Me, and I will answer him; I will be with him in trouble; I will deliver him and honor him. With long life I will satisfy him, and show him My salvation" (Psalm 91:13-16).

Daniel and his three friends were put to the ultimate test: Deny God or die. Shadrach, Meshach and Abed-Nego faced the fiery furnace. Daniel had his den of lions. Though they set their hearts to face death and were ready to pay the greatest price to remain faithful to Him, they were supernaturally delivered as a testimony. Jesus came into the place of terror with them.

Not all tests are lions. God has promised to keep us from the *lion* (the unavoidable problem), the *adder* (the unexpected attack) and the *dragon* (the unearthly assault). Whatever the terror of the time, we have His promise of His presence, His power and His deliverance. He *will* be with us.

So, how *do* you face the ultimate test? God has not promised us that we would not die. All of us die. Some of us die sooner than others. The only difference in death between a Christian and one who is not is that the Christian is ready to meet Jesus. *A Christian is dead already*—dead to the world, *but alive to Christ*. Death for you as a child of God is to fall asleep in His arms and awake in the other world, alive forever beyond the power of pain, safe forever from all sickness and suffering (see 1 Thessalonians 4:13; 1 Corinthians 15:49-55; 5:1-9).

Daniel and his friends fully knew the cost of loving God and staying true to Him. Faced with the horror of an agonizing death, they did not flinch or turn back. And in both cases, they experienced a wonderful, supernatural intervention. Each time, God showed up in a way that made even the king worship the one and only Creator of the universe. From Daniel we can learn three important tactics should you have to face your own "den of lions" some day:

1. *Innocence.* Keep your heart pure. When Daniel came out of the den, he said God had shut the lions' mouths because Daniel

was "found innocent before Him" (Daniel 6:22). Don't ever go into a lion's den without a *clean heart*. Get clean from all known sin. When they lowered Daniel into that pit, he knew only one thing for certain: His heart was wholly right with God. (See also Matthew 5:8; Psalms 24:3-5; 51:6-13.)

2. *Forgiveness*. Even though the king's own foolishness and pride had resulted in a death sentence for Daniel, Daniel held no grudges. Study his response. There is no railing against the king, no bitterness, no divine-judgement death threats (see Daniel 6:16-22). Paul and Silas in prison were unjustly whipped and beaten. Yet when the earthquake came, they stayed to save the jailer and his family. They could have said, "This is God; let's split." Instead they said, "This is God. Let's stay" (see Acts 16:25-35). Go into the lion's den *fully forgiving* those who have done you wrong. (See also Luke 23:34; Acts 7:59,60.)

3. *Trust in the Lord*. The bottom line for every den of lions is "Trust God or die." For some it will be "Trust God *and* die." Whatever the outcome, when you face your crisis, you must go in trusting in nothing and no one except the Sovereign Living God (see Daniel 6:23).

> I will say of the Lord, "He is my refuge and my fortress; my God, in Him I will trust." Surely He shall deliver you from the snare of the fowler and from the perilous pestilence. He shall cover you with His feathers, and under His wings you shall take refuge; His truth shall be your shield and buckler.
>
> You shall not be afraid of the terror by night, nor of the arrow that flies by day, nor of the pestilence that walks in darkness, nor of the destruction that lays waste at noonday.
>
> A thousand may fall at your side, and ten thousand at your right hand; but it shall not come near you. Only with your eyes shall you look, and see the reward of the wicked.

Because you have made the Lord, who is my refuge,
even the Most High, your dwelling place, no evil shall
befall you, nor shall any plague come near your dwelling;
for He shall give His angels charge over you, to keep you
in all your ways (Psalm 91:2-11).

NOTE

1. Paul Cain and Rick Joyner, "The Clinton Administration; Its Meaning and
   Our Future," *MorningStar Prophetic Bulletin*, January 1993, p. 3. The bulletin
   also contains a stern rebuke to the Church for holding critical and judge-
   mental attitudes of spiritual intolerance (see Proverbs 6:16-19) and trying to
   win spiritual battles by the carnal weapons of numerical might and political
   scheming, as well as a scriptural challenge to pray biblically for our government.

PART II

ANATOMY OF AN AWAKENING

WHAT IN HEAVEN'S NAME IS HAPPENING?

It ought to be apparent to all but the hermit and the willfully ignorant that something of *momentous proportions* is happening in our time. Newspapers and magazines like *Time, Newsweek* and *USA Today* carry articles on the awakening in churches, and talk shows like "Good Morning, America," "The Tonight Show" and "Politically Incorrect" have a new topic on their breaking-news list: REVIVAL. From the United States, Mexico, Latin America, China, Eastern Europe, Korea, India, Britain and the Pacific are coming strange stories of God dealing with people in some very unusual ways.

What is going on?

PROPHECY TEACHERS OR PROPHETIC TEACHERS?

Awakenings may arrive in a spiritual vacuum, but they never happen in an historical void. Each one has a silhouette, a structure, a stamp to it—a divine shaping from heaven fitted to the specifics of the spiritual war of the time and to those who must fight it for Him. It is easy to look back on what has gone before and to analyze an awakening in retrospect. But as A. W. Tozer pointed out, the trick is to see it while it is still coming:

The prophet is one who knows his times and what God is trying to say to the people of his times. . . . Today we need prophetic preachers; not preachers of prophecy but preachers with a gift of prophecy. The word of wisdom is missing. We need the gift of discernment again in our pulpits. It is not the ability to predict that we need, but the anointed eye, the power of spiritual penetration and interpretation, the ability to appraise the religious scene as viewed from God's perspective and to tell us what is actually going on.

What is needed desperately today is prophetic insight. Scholars can interpret the past; it takes prophets to interpret the present. Learning will enable a man to pass judgement on our yesterdays; but it requires a gift of clear seeing to pass sentence on our own day. One hundred years from now, historians will know what was taking place religiously in this year of our Lord; but that will be too late for us. We need to know right now (*Of God and Men*, pp. 20, 21).

What can we learn from God's work in history? As Francis Schaeffer noted, God's revealed will is true but never exhaustive. We are like little children with a big bunch of colorful balloons. We can get our fingers around all the strings, but when we look up, we can only see a few of the balloons at a time. What God shows us will be real, but He never shows us everything. Jesus said to the disciples, "I still have many things to say to you, but you cannot bear them now" (John 16:12).

What God does show our human family in reformation and revival is sufficient and progressive. His work is wondrous now, but it will go on. In the nature of redemption something fully redeemed need not be yet completed. Each visitation in history truly meets needs in its time, but an infinite God has more gifts to give. He is the great *I am*, not the great *I was*.

But we can learn from what He has done in the whole Church over the centuries. A well-known contemporary preacher was roundly criticized for some of his theology, and he went to the Lord over it. He said, "Lord, I'm so tired of being attacked over what I preach. I want to know the whole counsel of God."

God said to him, "I put it in the rest of the Body of Christ. *Go ask them.*"

We can expect from the God of the Bible and of history a *continuous unfolding* to us of more and more facets of His awesome nature and character. As a beautiful rose exists already inside the initial bud, waiting to develop in due time, all God's true works have much more in them than meets the eye at present. Angels have watched the One who sits on the throne for millennia, but they never get bored. Every moment, every hour, there is something wonderful and new to see in Him. That is why they cover their eyes and say, "Holy, holy, holy!" (Revelation 4:8).

Seeing the Present in the Past: Historical Revival

Each awakening throughout history has had a *shape*, a *structure* and a *purpose*. From the Reformation to the Third Wave Movement up to the New Millennium, we see in His ways and works an unfolding revelation of His nature and character in the nature and character of His salvation.

After centuries of spiritual darkness when the Church—seeking wealth, control and status—to a large extent lost its way, its soul and its spiritual power, the Reformation was the light of a new dawn. Men like Huss and Wycliffe died at the stake for the Scriptures. Others like Luther, with a conscience chained to truth, dared to defy the entrenched might of a corrupt Church to bring back the recovery of Scriptures, the centrality of faith, liberty of conscience and the priesthood of all believers.

Where would we be today without the right to hold our own Bible studies, to share a personal relationship with Christ, to enjoy the privilege of hearing God's voice for ourselves, to know true community in believers' fellowship? God spoke these truths to men who hazarded their lives to bring them back to the Church. We ignore them to our loss; we lose them to our spiritual peril.[1]

Tough and crusty old Reformers, standing up with grits and guts to the religious nonsense and political power of the day, returned to the people a trustworthy Bible and certain foundational truths. These were rough men raised up for rough times. Their song was "A Mighty Fortress Is Our God," and they put back in place the planks of a platform upon which the Church could stand against the winds of the world.

Yet when the Pilgrim fathers first came to America seeking to put these principles into practice in a nation, their pastor John Robinson reminded them:

> We have come to a period in religion (when) the Lutherans cannot be drawn beyond what Luther saw. And the Calvinists stick where Calvin left them. Luther and Calvin were precious shining lights in their times, yet God did not reveal His whole will to them. I am very confident that the Lord has yet more truth and light to break forth out of His Holy Word (George Fry and Duane Arnold, "Reclaiming Reformation Day," *Christianity Today*, October 1982, p. 36).

During the next two awesome centuries, the Church saw the manifested power of the First and Second Great Awakenings, up to and including the 1858 revival. All were escalating demonstrations of the greatness and glory of God at work in His people. While building on the strengths of the Reformation, the revivalists corrected some of its weaknesses.

They held Reform convictions of the absolute authenticity and inspiration of Scripture. They did not forget the great truths of justification by faith, the lordship of Christ and the sovereignty of God. They had learned the call to discipline and holiness as true children of God. But these next-generation believers went a step further than the Reformers were able to go: They restored neglected facets of the gospel that we still need today.

THE FIRST AWAKENING

The First Awakening followed the Reformation under Zinzendorf, Whitfield, Wesley and others. The Moravians sent teams of young missionaries into the world to win the lost and save the Church. Crowds of up to 50,000 came out to hear young Whitfield preach, "You must be born again!" Wesley's itinerant bands preached and taught with power, saving England under God from what happened to *les misérables* in the aftermath of the French Revolution.

They were a kinder, gentler breed, these seventeenth-century revivalists and open-air preachers. They learned from the shortcomings of their predecessors. Although attacked both in print and in person, their reply was not with physical sword and fire, but with intense Scripture testimony and *supernatural* power. Now their refrain was "Be of sin the double cure; cleanse me from its guilt and power" and "My chains fell off, my soul was free; I rose went forth and followed Thee." Practical holiness of heart and life, the responsibility of the believer in witness and the gospel work of the Kingdom were their themes, and they affected forever the shape of evangelism.

THE SECOND AWAKENING

The Second Awakening, under God's servants like Jonathan Edwards and Charles Finney, extended even further the boundaries of spiritual and social change. Jeremiah Lamphier called for city prayer in the 1858 aftermath of a great depression; men like

Kier Hardy and Lord Shaftesbury fought for reform of labor among children and adults; George Mueller and Dr. Barnado loved orphans in the name of Christ; caring Christians raised up the Red Cross; and revivalist George Williams founded the Young Men's Christian Association (YMCA).

Even slavery was finally brought to the anvil of God. Chains were broken across two continents, although this time the cost was a terrible civil war that pitted brother against brother. D. L. Moody, the shoe salesman, made souls his business; William and Catherine Booth founded the Salvation Army and took compassion to the streets, where the song of the saints was "Send the Fire" and "Throw Out the Lifeline."[2]

Wesley and Whitfield, Finney and Edwards, Lamphier and Moody. Many such friends and brothers in both Awakenings attempted to prepare the world for Jesus to rule in it again. Though much more evangelistic, compassionate and certainly more Christ-like in practical character than some of the earlier saints, they still did not live long enough to see a full flowering of many things they experienced in their lives and knew God would do. Power to be *free*, power to *live clean* and power to *affect the world*—they saw them all begin to really happen as the pillar of fire moved on. It was plain the work of God was not finished.

TWENTIETH-CENTURY MOBILIZATION

Fast-forward now to the dawn of the twentieth century and witness the divine mobilization of the Church to world missions and supernatural equipping for the unfinished task. Evan Roberts heard the wind of God on his heart in the 1904 Welsh revival; Willie Seymour bowed beneath it on Asuza Street; Billy Graham took the gospel to the cities and the nations, and a mass outpouring of healing and saving power began on a whole new level among the nations of the world.

In the accelerating events of the latter part of this century, God has revealed yet more of His awesome nature, restoring the sense of His *supernatural presence*, allowing Him due worship in spirit and truth, and *demonstrated power*, healing a physically and morally sick world.

SEEING THE FUTURE IN THE PRESENT: CONTEMPORARY VISITATION

God is not just after local homes and churches. The whole earth is His and is to declare His rightful glory. What signs are we seeing that God is at work all over the world in an unprecedented way?

Spiritual Op Centers. Teams of Christians are now targeting spiritual strongholds all over the world. Focused prayer, unified intercession and spiritually and statistically informed research groups are networking new war zones. Thousands are praying step-by-step through geographical windows, standing in the gap for whole nations and peoples and praying the Lord of the harvest to raise up laborers.

Reconciliation Movements. Christians worldwide are walking in the steps of past tragedies and atrocities, meeting leaders and previously untouched peoples to identify in tears and repentance the past failures of the Church to be like Jesus and, as a result, are seeing real healing and reconciliation.

Extraordinary Prayer/Unity. Citywide, nationwide and global calls for fasting and prayer are finding answering chords of response in Christian leaders willing to cooperate to see awakening in their nations.

Unusual Visitations. Villages and towns are seeing patently supernatural evidences of the reality and power of Christ as Jesus reveals Himself in unmistakable ways to hungry unbelievers.

Global Impact. Entire nations are being affected by the gospel[3], and national leaders are declaring the rulership of Christ in their people.[4] Even the very weather of the world seems to speak of the day when a sad and groaning creation will be set free to celebrate the victory of the sons and daughters of the living God.

Thus we come to the edge of contemporary history, one that begins at the dawn of the twenty-first century. It leads to what some believe may be completed in your lifetime—His last and greatest demonstration of His glory.

NOTES

1. Reformers won back ground for some central foundations from which all true revival flows: *true spirituality* that flows from the grace of **free justification by faith** (see Habakkuk 2:4; Romans 1:17; Galatians 3:11; Hebrews 10:38), *biblical authority* out of the **lordship of Christ** (see 1 Chronicles 16:31; Psalms 33:12; 96:10; Isaiah 43:10; John 15:16; 2 Thessalonians 2:13) and that sense of *divine destiny* drawn from a vision of **God's sovereign reign** in history (see Psalm 97:1; see also Psalm 99; 103:19; 2 Chronicles 20:6; Ephesians 1:4; 2 Timothy 1:9; 1 Peter 2:9; 2 Peter 1:10; 1 Corinthians 1:26-28; Revelation 17:14).
2. The shape of these First and Second Awakenings included added emphasis on the **obligation of man**, or *responsibility* (see Joshua 24:15; 1 Chronicles 28:9; 2 Chronicles 7:14; 16:9; Psalms 24:3-6; 71:18; 119:2; Isaiah 55:6; John 8:36; Acts 17:27; Romans 8:2; 2 Corinthians 3:17; Hebrews 11:6); **holiness before the Lord**, or *purity* (see Deuteronomy 18:13; 1 Chronicles 28:9; Psalm 110:3; Isaiah 35:8; Matthew 5:48; Romans 6:22; 2 Corinthians 7:1; 1 Thessalonians 3:13; Hebrews 7:19; 12:14; 13:21; 1 Peter 5:10); and the **work of the kingdom**, or *ministry* (see Isaiah 61:1; Micah 3:8; Zechariah 4:6; Matthew 24:14; Luke 1:17; 4:18; Acts 1:8; 1 John 3:17).
3. Bill Gothard speaks of the key biblical principle of being a people "zealous of good works" in gaining the respect and attention of a whole nation for Christian training. There are three keys to opening such a door: (1) Show them first the fruit especially in the lives of holy young people transformed by the true gospel; (2) Don't mind who gets the credit as long as God gets the glory; and (3) Don't charge them for anything; let it be a completely free gift.
4. Recent elections of men like J. T. Chiluba of Zambia are examples of unashamed international witnesses to Christ. On his election to the presidency of his nation, Chiluba publicly consecrated the country to Jesus Christ. Since the onset of his presidency, the economy has begun to recover, many government officials have become genuine Christians and the long-withheld rains so essential for economic survival have begun again.

PART III

DIVINE PREPARATION
FOR DESTINY

THE SET-UPS OF GOD

Because the foolishness of God is wiser than men,
and the weakness of God is stronger than men. For
you see your calling, brethren, that not many wise
according to the flesh, not many mighty, not many
noble, are called. But God has chosen the foolish
things of the world to put to shame the wise, and
God has chosen the weak things of the world to put
to shame the things which are mighty; and the base
things of the world and the things which are despised
God has chosen, and the things which are not, to
bring to nothing the things that are, that no flesh
should glory in His presence. But of Him you are in
Christ Jesus, who became for us wisdom from God—
and righteousness and sanctification and
redemption—that, as it is written, "He who glories,
let him glory in the Lord."

1 Corinthians 1:25-31

If God made movies instead of history, He as the Ultimate Writer-Director would work from His own great script. Drafted long before the film, it would demonstrate His talent, creativity and skill. He could handpick actors for the characters and parts He wanted played, yet give them freedom to enter into the role for which each was chosen. He, however, would control all the key scenes of the plot—for example, how each part relates to the others, or how the beginning of the film is tied in to the end. If an actor failed to show up or continually blew his lines, the Director could even replace him and redo the scene.

Of course, history is not a movie and life is not a play. You can't change a movie once completed and on the screen. Yet we note that the book of Acts has no "Amen" at the end of it, because the work of God goes on and human history (which is really His-story) is still not finished. At least, not yet.

God Is Smarter Than You Are: Of Fish and Fire

Now the servants and officers who had made a fire of coals stood there, for it was cold, and they warmed themselves. And Peter stood with them and warmed himself (John 18:18).

Then, as soon as they had come to land, they saw a fire of coals there, and fish laid on it, and bread (John 21:9).

When the Lord called Simon Peter to follow Him by the side of the sea, He got Simon's attention with a huge catch of fish—on the very day this resident expert had caught nothing. It was not a sermon that caught his attention, but the fish in the net that showed him he was a sinner. For a little more than three years, Simon Peter followed this Jesus, learning how to be a "fisher of men," but it wasn't always easy. He was certainly flabbergasted when Jesus called him a stone—the rock upon which He would build His Church—then just moments later addressed him as "Satan" himself (see Matthew 16:13-23). Then there was his failure on the Sea of Galilee (see Matthew 14:22-31). It's hard to put your money where your mouth is when you see Jesus walking toward you on the heaving, churning water and hear Him calling, "Come."

Then came that terrible day when Christ was betrayed and taken, when the flame of the Roman fire was not enough to touch the cold terror Peter felt at the thought of what was sure to be his own imminent arrest and execution. The Big Fisherman used words he thought he had forgotten. He cursed and swore (see Matthew 26:74) and denied he ever knew the One being sentenced as he spoke—the One he had sworn he would never forsake or leave. On that day, it was the crowing of the cock and the glance of God as it happened that broke Simon Peter's heart, and he went out into the night and wept (see Luke 22:61,62).

It took a special word from an angel of the Lord for the women at the tomb to stop him from walking away forever: "Go, tell His disciples—*and Peter*" (Mark 16:7). Yet even after the Resurrection, Peter was weary. One dull day he announced to the others he was returning to his old life: "I go fishing." Some agreed: "We go with you." And on that day, just like when he met Jesus three years earlier, he caught nothing (see John 21:3-6).

Then there appeared a stranger on the shore, calling to them, asking in all innocence, "Children, did you catch anything? Cast your net on the other side of the boat." And then there came an explosion of fish that began to sink the boat, and Peter, forever God's Fisherman, knew who that Figure was (see John 21:7).

Do you believe in the set-ups of God?

THE UGLY DUCKLING: LOSERS INTO LEADERS

And the Lord said to Satan, "The Lord rebuke you, Satan! The Lord who has chosen Jerusalem rebuke you! Is this not a brand plucked from the fire?" (Zechariah 3:2).

By all media accounts, Generation Xers and GenNexters have been deservedly shafted. They have been labeled the biggest bunch of losers in contemporary society. The social pundits and prophets of secularity have written these kids off as the worst of the West, a generation without ambition, dreams or means. They've grown up in a world on the edge of social safety-net collapse, doomed to holding down a McJob and living with their parents forever. But remember the story of the Ugly Duckling. Some fairy tales come true.

"HE ESTABLISHED A TESTIMONY"

The first thing on God's agenda when He sets about changing history is to *establish a testimony*. Where there is no vision, the people perish. God always begins with something you can see in someone you can touch.

His purpose is to incarnate His Son in us again through the miracle of the new birth. Jesus said to His disciples, "I have to leave now so the Holy Spirit can come" (see John 16:7). He ascended into heaven and sent His Spirit to dwell in and work through His people. The Holy Spirit was to the Early Church what Jesus was to His disciples in person. But instead of being in just one place, He can now be in millions.

If Jesus had stayed and not gone away He could only live in one place, perhaps somewhere like the Vatican, and you might only get to watch Him on TV or in a rare public appearance. His strategy for retaking His world is simple and has always been the same: *to demonstrate who He is by planting people who love Him into an arena of "lostness."* The kingdom of God is founded on friendship; His plans are people. That is what the Church is supposed to be: people who show His life, His love and His power.

He likes to have at least two or three. If there is only one of you, people may know that you are different, may even know that you are holy and belong to another world. But you might also be just one in a million. You might—like John Travolta in *Phenomenon*—be that misunderstood, special individual who only appears once in a generation to challenge our ideas of what is real and normal. But God's plan is to use all kinds of different people who don't look anything like each other but who all look something like Him. Red and yellow, black and white. Smart and simple, wealthy and poor. Old and young, tall and short. Pretty and plain, from every tongue, tribe, nation and people group on earth we are called to represent Him.

History shows that His favorite plan is to lay His hand on someone everyone else has written off or ignored. He likes it like that. God took a great risk when He made creation outside of Himself. He took an even greater risk when He made man in His image and likeness—a mankind that could break its promise and break His heart. He took a still greater risk when He became a man Himself. He took on the biological life of His own creation and lived a perfect life among us. It was a supreme risk, to lay down that precious life for us on the Cross at the hill called Calvary. But the greatest risk God ever took in all of history is the one He takes now—*letting people like you and me represent Him.*

God has always chosen to use the very people most of history would vote least likely to succeed. Who is Israel, after all? What is there about this tiny nation—so small you can cover it with a thumbtack on a map of the world—and its inhabitants who have been in the headlines of history for thousands of years? What explanation is there that such a small country with less than one percent of the world's population should own more than one-fifth of all Nobel prizes, its people continually at the forefront of fields as diverse as the military, economics, industry, science, culture, music, drama and comedy?

There is only one real answer: Thousands of years ago, God

chose to hang out with them. Prior to that time, Israel's ancestors were not a great people. As big a loser as any of the nations that surrounded them (all of which have long since perished from the face of the earth), their biological, cultural or merely religious origins are not the explanation. The true answer to the enigma of Israel is not genetic, scientific or educational.

The answer to Israel is simple: God.

They were a chosen people. His presence made them awesome. They were not chosen because they were special. *They were special because they were chosen.*

God has not changed His preference for losers. God loves it when experts write off a person or a generation as a hopeless, useless, worthless cause. He delights in taking those others call losers and making them leaders to show His power and presence. Count the losers of Israel's history. Sometimes He had to show them their failure before they were fit to lead.

Look who He established a testimony in—*Jacob* (see Psalm 78:5).

WHO WAS JACOB?
If you had been there to pick the boy most likely to succeed out of Isaac's sons, would you have picked Jacob? Here is big, hairy-chested Esau, the kind of guy you don't want to line up against on a football field. The sort of dude whose idea of a fun day out is to hunt down and kill Bambi. And over in the other corner is weedy, geeky, not-yet-shaving Jacob who helps Mummy do the dishes. Think Arnold Schwarzenegger and Danny DeVito in *Twins.* Who would you pick to be the future ruler and representative of a nation?

Isaac *thought* he knew. The Bible puts it this way: "And Isaac loved Esau . . . but Rebekah loved Jacob" (Genesis 25:28). And who did God pick? "The elder shall serve the younger" (Genesis 25:23, *KJV*). Time and time again God boasts about Jacob, the one who was later to be called Israel. *God established a testimony in Jacob.*

WHO WAS MOSES?

Of course, we know who Moses was. Prince of Egypt. Greatest lawgiver in Israel's history. The guy who got in the face of Pharaoh, the most powerful man in the world, and delivered a nation out of bondage. The one who talked to God face-to-face as a man speaks to his friend.

Moses was also a holocaust survivor, the only child spared from a vicious pogrom against a generation of babies, brought up in the palace of the Adolf Hitler of his time, trained to be a Pharaoh.

And how did he do? Well, he failed his first test of deliverance. He murdered the man he was witnessing to and was forced to flee into the desert and hide out for forty long years with a bunch of pungent sheep in the desert sun. He certainly looked like a real long-term loser. So what changed Moses? An encounter with God in a burning bush, the same God who had spared his life and protected him from his childhood for a purpose (see Exodus 3).

From a man trained to think, talk and walk like an Egyptian, Moses became one who, when he was come of age, refused to be called the son of Pharaoh's daughter, choosing rather to suffer affliction with the people of God (see Hebrews 11:24,25). Was he a fool? He could have been Pharaoh! He could have had his own pyramid and his own gold coffin. He could have been famous. Instead he cast his lot with a crazy band of people that hardly *wanted* to escape from bondage, a people who complained so much that Moses struck the rock and died himself like so many had already done in the wilderness (see Numbers 20:7-13). Was he a fool?

Centuries later, three fishermen watched in terror as a cloud came down over the mountain where they had gone to pray with Jesus. On that unspeakably terrifying day when they heard the voice of God and fell down almost unconscious with fright, they saw standing with Jesus the prophet Elijah and someone else who had made it onto the mountain. And who was this figure with

Elijah, the greatest of the prophets, standing also in splendor by Jesus? Not a rotting mummy propped up or bandaged and put on display for exhibition, carried from town to town to show the glory that once was Egypt, but a live, transfigured Moses, who made it into the Promised Land just as God had said, a little late but truly there as promised by the One who called him so long before (see Luke 9:27-31).

Moses made his choice; Pharaoh made his. You tell me who was the final loser. At the end of time, they sing the song of Moses and the Lamb.

WHO WAS PETER?

Peter is probably not the kind of guy you or I would have picked to take up on the mountain with us to see Moses and Elijah. Peter was the disciple with the foot-shaped mouth, the only disciple with the dubious distinction of being interrupted by all three members of the Godhead at one time or another during his ministry. He's the one who cursed Jesus and denied he ever knew Him before the crucifixion, the one who headed off to backslide into his pre-disciple fishing business even *after* Jesus rose from the dead. Let me ask you, *Would you have picked a loser like Peter to be a leader in the Church?*

WHO WAS PAUL?

Who would you have picked as the man to head up the Early Church missions movement and write half the New Testament? How about a Pharisee of the Pharisees? How about an arrogant, proud, intensely religious zealot utterly opposed to everything connected to Christianity? How about someone who not only hated Christians but also whose itinerant ministry might have been called "Kill Christians for God"? Would you have picked such a man to carry the torch for Jesus? Would you even trust him to hold a Bible study for your home fellowship? No wonder the early Christians found it hard to believe he was actually saved.

Nero finally caught him, put him in prison and cut off his head. Now we call our dogs "Nero" and our sons "Paul."

Any pulpit committee would outright reject most of the men God has used to change nations. Consider their qualifications:

- Noah had 120 years of preaching experience *without a single convert.*
- Enoch was okay, but one day he went out for a walk—with God, he said—and never came back.
- Abraham took off for Egypt during hard times, got into trouble with the authorities and tried to lie his way out of it.
- Solomon had a reputation for incredible wisdom, but failed to practice what he preached.
- Elijah proved to be inconsistent and folded under pressure.
- Hosea's family life was a shambles. He married a hooker and couldn't keep her.
- Jeremiah was emotional and something of an alarmist.
- Amos came from a farming background.
- John *said* he was a Baptist, but lacked tact, dressed like a hippie and would stick out like a sore thumb at a church potluck.
- Timothy had potential, but was considered by some to be much too young for a pastoral position.

And Jesus! Jesus is out of the question. He frequently offended church members, especially seminary graduates. He upset the first selection committee that ever heard Him, so much so they drove Him out of the church and tried to push Him over a cliff and stone Him (see Luke 4:16-30). He ruined the whole service! No wonder they didn't take up an offering for Him.

God hath chosen the foolish things of the world to confound the wise (1 Corinthians 1:27, *KJV*).

Perhaps one of the reasons why the youth of today are so special to God is that others have written them off as the biggest losers in contemporary history. He loves it when people who do not know His heart (and don't give a rip for a people He has purposed to make awesome) see in astonishment what He does with those they never wanted. With such an army of losers, with a company of those perennially left behind, left unloved and left out, He can show His glory to the world.

INUNDATED BY HELL: BURNED BY EVERYONE AND EVERYTHING

For my days are consumed like smoke, and my bones
are burned like a hearth. My heart is stricken and
withered like grass, so that I forget to eat my bread.
Because of the sound of my groaning my
bones cling to my skin.

Psalm 102:3-5

And he saw his days burn up like paper in fire.

— John Cougar Mellencamp
"Paper in Fire"

Crap like drugs, crime, sexual disease and family
stress is all stuff you blame us for, when you were the
ones that raised them all to an art form. You blame
the young for having no concept of the higher ideals
in life, when you were the ones who trashed most of
them. You dived into this selfish, flaky, hippie drug
philosophy when it was hip, then did a 180 and
accuse us of having a short attention span!

— "Crasher" on U. S. Talk Net

This is a *survivor* generation—GenXers still alive to face the war against them are the lucky ones. *One third of Generation X never even made it into the world.* They were killed before they were born. *Sixteen million* GenXers died without a chance to even understand what was happening to them, deliberately aborted by their parents.

Those who survived the war on the womb were forced to live through the breakdown of the nuclear family. Another 16 million managed to survive parents' divorces, often multiple times on both sides of the family.

Many a mom took solace in prescription Prozacs, fantasy soap operas or daytime talk shows detailing lurid and crazy relationships and lifestyles that made hers look almost normal. Others found "fulfillment" amid the competitive politics of the workplace, often as the only alternative to a miserable marriage.

Dads did no better. Many either split or lost themselves in their work. Others kept a lover on the side or took out their pent-up frustrations on their own families. Four out of ten girls of GenX were abused physically, sexually or emotionally.

No wonder they're called Generation X. It must have often seemed to them that the whole world was out to hurt them, blame them or kill them.

"HE APPOINTED A LAW"

I'd like to know who makes the rules, who sets the rules (Duchess Sarah Ferguson on "Good Morning, America," October 13, 1998).

After establishing a testimony, the second thing God does when He sets out to take back His world is to *appoint law*. In a culture where all beliefs are accepted, where there are no longer any absolutes and no one thing is more important than another, people become crazy and live selfishly.

Think of it. Do we really want to live as if everything is true? As if nothing is bigger than our own ideas and nothing is more important than anything else? When a land gives up the idea of divine law, it must make up its own. When Israel as a nation went down the tubes in the past—which it did repeatedly—it did so in four stages:

1. Israel forgot about *God* (see Deuteronomy 6:12; 8:11-20; Job 8:8-15; Psalms 9:17; 50:14-23; 106:21; Jeremiah 2:31,32).
2. Israel forgot God's *laws* (see Deuteronomy 4:5-9,23-28; 2 Kings 17:38; Psalms 78:36,37; 103:2,17,18; Proverbs 3:1,2).
3. Israel worshiped *new gods* (see Deuteronomy 4:15-19,23-28; Jeremiah 2:11-13,26-28; 23:24-27).
4. Israel made up *new laws* (see Psalm 106:21,28,29,39; Judges 17:6; Romans 1:30).

"So the children of Israel did evil in the sight of the Lord. They forgot the Lord their God, and served the Baals and Asherahs" (Judges 3:7). They forgot God, forgot His laws, worshiped new gods and made up new laws. So did Israel fall.

So, how do we decide what is true today? We *vote*—what Francis Schaeffer used to call "the dictatorship of the 51 percent." If just over half the people believe something is true, it becomes true.

I have in my lab in New Zealand a bottle of cyanide. (All chemists have cyanide.) I keep it in a place that is hard to reach. The label on the bottle says in large red letters, "POISON: Not to Be Taken." Now cyanide is one of the deadliest chemicals around. It kills by strangling your blood cells to death within seconds of ingestion. Yet of all the chemicals in my lab, sodium cyanide is one of the nicest smelling. It smells like almonds.

What if I took that bottle and put a new label on it? Say,

ALMOND JELLY BEANS. If you ate it, you would still die instantly. But you wouldn't know *why*. The label does not *create* what is in the bottle; it simply *defines* it.

God's laws are not inventions. They are not made up, as if God said, "I need some rights and wrongs. Let's call these 5,000 things right and these 5,000 things wrong. Wait a minute, that's far too many rights and not enough wrongs. Let's make it 7,500 wrongs and 2,500 rights." Even God does not invent right and wrong. Truth and right are founded in His own changeless being. God's laws are merely *descriptions of true reality*. They tell us from His perspective what is truly right and fit and good.

In our crazy culture, we think we can determine for ourselves what is right and wrong without knowing all the facts and without seeing the whole picture. We think we can live happily and sanely without an infinite reference point. We are like people who have caught a serious disease. Most of us have developed a fever of 104 degrees, so we collect data, average the results, decide what is *now* normal and then *recalibrate the thermometer*. Everyone still dies, but nobody knows why.

One European nation decided to decriminalize certain sexual acts that before had been illegal. Some months after the grand experiment, the government announced that sexual crime had dropped considerably. This suggests a way to do away with crime completely. Simply decriminalize everything! People will still get hurt and die, but it won't be wrong anymore.

God *appointed a law* in Israel (see Psalm 78:5). In wisdom and kindness, He tells us what is right and good and what is stupid and wrong. This is a generation that has learned—often the hard way—that many of the things people think are all right for some will often hurt everyone in the long run. Almost by default, they are rediscovering the truth of the law of God. We can discover it, do it and live; or we can reject it and be destroyed as individuals, families and nations.

God is only after two things for your life—that you be happy and holy. And He knows you cannot be really happy until you are holy.

IGNORED BY THE CHURCH: PELICANS, OWLS AND OTHER ODD BIRDS

> Your hideous obsession with celebrities, beauty and youth have made every single one of my friends convinced they are ugly and worthless. . . . Maybe I'm being irrational, but there's just something about your Baby Boomer mentality that makes me want to burn down the magazine rack at the supermarket ("Crasher," U. S. Talk Net).

> I am like a pelican of the wilderness: I am like an owl of the desert. I watch, and am as a sparrow alone upon the house top (Psalm 102:6,7, *KJV*).

Some of God's most bizarre creatures are birds. A visit to any aviary, pet shop or zoo will give you revelation if you look long enough.

Pelicans in the heavens look cool. But on the ground it's obvious they have the most peculiar faces. Sporting big, waddly bags under their stiff upper lips to keep their lunch in, they strut around on outlandish legs looking like some poncy character from a Monty Python movie.

Owls, true creatures of the night, sound weird and have the scariest eyes. Their heads even rotate like in *The Exorcist* when they want to look backwards. Born with skewed direction-finding hearing equipment essential for their survival, only two tufts of feathers like a toupee of fake ears keep them from imminent self-rejection.

And sparrows? Nobody even notices sparrows. Eagles we know, hummingbirds we know, even turkeys we know, but who ever sees a sparrow? Who gives a rip about a common, little brown bird that is not at all in any way special? Yet God attends the funeral of each sparrow (see Matthew 10:29), and what we laugh at or ignore, He made with a divine purpose and He loves.

Nobody seems to notice kids either. They are the largely invisible segment of the congregation, only noticed when they make themselves a nuisance or are no longer there. As in other areas of life, a great deal of church activity is oddly focused on the older generations, those people *least likely to get saved*. The average age of conversion today in the United States is *15 years old*. Some 67 percent of all people saved are getting saved before they reach the age of 18. Eighty percent of all conversions take place by the age of 24. By the age of 39, *90 percent of all who will be saved in this nation have already been saved*.

Put it another way: Once you leave the years of the young, you only have one chance in ten of ever becoming a Christian at all. Growing old in sin is key evidence of reprobation.

> **Item:** A detailed survey of British churches in the past decade before the revival showed the scary statistical loss from the church of an average of some 300 young people per week. That same year, in one of the major Spring Harvest Conventions, the churches put 300 teens from the youth section of the convention into the main meeting to join with the adults for worship. Near the end of the singing, they pulled them out, leaving the adults alone again to sing on without them. The comment made by the adults after they left: "It felt like a funeral."

Pastors and ministers sometimes say, "We need to take care of our young people. They are the future of the Church."

I tell them, "Wake up, Pastor. They are not the 'future' of the

Church. They *are* the Church. If you don't commit a corresponding-
ly significant portion of your prayer, focus and budget to
them, you can kiss good-bye your church and ministry, future or
not."

Study the records of Scripture and Church history. Although
God usually uses mature saints to direct, guide and shepherd
young converts, the actual harvest is cultivated from the young in
every generation. This is not only true of this time; it is more truly
so now than in any other generation.

Greg Johnson has pointed out that you are only a teenager
for seven years (13 through 19). If you survive, you may well be an
adult ten times longer. Greg's challenge to what he calls the
"Youth Church" is this: "Give God the tithe of your teenage years
and He will give you an open heaven for the rest of your life."

The Beast was not always a beast.

He rejected a witch one day and a curse came on his life that
turned him ugly. He would remain a hideous beast until there
came someone who, despite the way he looked, would love him
for what he was. And Beauty did come, and he really loved her.
But only when the Beast was willing to give up his own life to save
her was he forever transformed into what he was always meant to
be.

One of the beautiful new worship choruses today was given
to an older Christian woman in answer to her lonely prayer.
Feeling the fleeting nature of time and her own frustration in not
seeming to have accomplished much in her life, she needed a real
word from the Lord for her heart. This is the song she got as an
answer to that prayer:

> You are the reason I live,
> You are the reason I move.
> You are the reason, You are the reason

You are the reason, it's You . . .
And after everything is over,
You'll be the song I sing forever.

— 100 Portraits, "The Reason"

The thing that makes this song so special is this: It is the song
the *Lord sang to her for her*, not just a song for her to sing to Him.
What is the heart of the purpose of Christ in all that He has done,
in all that He has wrought in all of history? The Church is His
beloved Bride, the one for whom He risked all and gave all. We are
the glory of His inheritance, the treasure of His heart. He paid the
ultimate price for His Church and now chooses to work through
us to show the world just how awesome and wonderful He really is.

INDICTED BY SOCIETY: BAD-MOUTHED, SHAMED AND TRASH-TALKED

Mine enemies reproach me all the day; and they that
are mad against me are sworn against me.

Psalm 102:8, *KJV*

The educational skills of this generation will not sur-
pass, equal or even approach those of their parents.

— Nation at Risk

This is a new breed that will never know true belief,
true beauty or true passion.

— Francis Fukuyama
The End of History and the Last Man

Like children of a divorce, they carry a hidden
question: Before they came along, the nation was
doing great. After they arrived, everything in the core
started going to hell. Part of being a 13er is to always
wonder: "What did I do to make so many angry or
mad or unhappy about me?"

— Neil Howe
13th Generation: Abort, Retry, Ignore, Fail?

What is it about this generation that makes it such a target of adult criticism and rejection? It's easy when you are grown up to speak of how much better life was "when I was your age." I tell parents, "You never were their age." I believe that in many ways there has never been a generation like this one, that in ways their parents may never understand they are facing pressures and stresses no generation of young people have ever had to face.

Then why do so many adults criticize or attack you instead of encourage you? Many times it is a reaction out of fear for what they think or suspect you will become because of what they already have.

In the old Family Films movie *Pay the Piper*, the story is told of a man who, while waiting to celebrate at home his daughter's high school graduation, learns to his shock and horror that both she and her boyfriend have been tragically killed in an automobile accident. They were both apparently drunk, and the car went out of control. She was his only child. Although the dad himself drinks, he sets out on an angry and bitter crusade to find who it was in town that sold liquor to his underage daughter. In the months that follow, he works night and day to bring to justice bars and nightclub owners that violate the law. Exhausted one night, he goes to unlock his own home bar to have a drink himself, his first one since he began his mission. As the cabinet opens, a piece of paper flutters to the ground. On it are these words: *Dear Daddy, I hope you don't mind. We borrowed one of your bottles to celebrate. Love, Your Daughter.*

Some adults think their children are stupid, that they are unable to learn anything. But they do learn. They learn a lot more than adults think they do. They just won't say—most times—that what they have seen already is *not* what they want to be. And all the words and emotions and arguments will not change the truth of what they have lived with and grown up with.

Fathers, provoke not your children to wrath, say the Scriptures (see Ephesians 6:4). The rod of your anger shall fail (see Proverbs 22:8).

THIS IS NOT YOUR FATHER'S REVIVAL

Some things you can inherit. Solomon did what his father had done, and God did for Solomon what He did for David.

> And David built there an altar to the Lord, and offered burnt offerings and peace offerings, and called on the Lord; and He answered him from heaven by fire on the altar of burnt offering (1 Chronicles 21:26).

> When Solomon had finished praying, fire came down from heaven and consumed the burnt offering and the sacrifices; and the glory of the Lord filled the temple (2 Chronicles 7:1).

Some things you can inherit from a godly heritage. For those of us whose family history was more of a bush or a weed than a spiritual tree, we can take comfort in the fact that being born again puts us into a much larger spiritual family.

We can learn from and draw from the walk with God others have taken before us. We also have the Bible, the story of the men and women to whom God showed Himself faithful despite their own backgrounds or failures or weaknesses. We can read of these and draw from the lineage of God's profiles of courage. "Every promise in the Book is mine," says the old song. "Every chapter, every verse, every line."

We have the records of Christian history too. There are biographies and journals and accounts of other saints of God we can identify with and learn from and take from them an inheritance as our own. *What did they do in response to His call and grace that gave them such power in God?*

You can also learn from your parents. This is true whether or not they have ever loved or served God. (This is true even if they were the exact *opposite* of what God says a parent ought to live like and be like.) Perhaps your parents have actually seen with their own eyes a visitation from God. Ask them to tell you about it, about what God did when they were young. Learn what you can, even learn from what they did *not* say or do *not* do now.

But this is not your father's revival.

What God is doing now is not primarily designed for them, but for *you*. What He does now will build on what He did before, but what He did before is not always the same as what He wants to do now. Record your own story, chronicle your own dealings with Christ, journal your own spiritual journey with Jesus. One day others may also learn from what you learn of Him at this time.

SOME THINGS YOU'VE GOT TO TAKE TO THE KING YOURSELF

First there was the generation without a cause, then the generation with too many causes, followed by the tired generation (Arthur Holmes, Professor of Philosophy, Wheaton College).

The difference between now and "back then" can be seen in the ER room of any major hospital today. Twenty years ago when a teenager was brought in in critical condition, they asked, "What happened to him?" Now they ask instead, "What did he do? What is he on?" *You* are considered responsible for whatever is wrong. And you *feel* responsible for everything that happens—*If it's bad, it must be my fault.*

One of the things that exasperates your parents is that you seem to "veg out" on them at times. "Why don't you get with the program?!" they demand to know. You, of course, learn that while you can get blamed for not getting the job done, there's not a lot of help out there when you have to do it. Many of you learned early that it was no use asking Mom for help with the homework, because she said, "Ask your father"; and Dad, if he was there at all, thought the math homework was written in Hindustani.

Most of what you face today you have to face on your own; no one else is going to do it for you. All too many of you have learned that you can't really count on adults coming through when you don't know what to do. Kids learn to cope, to make do, to check things out. They learn the "truth" from friends, from asking around, from the Net, from others. You learn to go on doggedly on your own.

It doesn't look as if it's going to be much different in the near future. You may just have to live with it, pressure and all. But that doesn't have to be a bad thing. There is One who can stand with you and help you get done what really must be done. He will never quit on you, never tell you to go away and not bother Him, never say He doesn't know how to help you or tell you you're stupid for trying what seems to be an impossible "loser" task.

Some things you can inherit, but others you just have to do.

And they said to me, "The survivors who are left from the captivity in the province are there in great distress and reproach. The wall of Jerusalem is also broken down, and its gates are burned with fire."

And I said to the king, "If it pleases the king, and if your servant has found favor in your sight, I ask that you send me to Judah, to the city of my fathers' tombs, that I may rebuild it."

Then I said to them, "You see the distress that we are in, how Jerusalem lies waste, and its gates are burned with fire. Come and let us build the wall of Jerusalem, that we may no longer be a reproach" (Nehemiah 1:3; 2:5,17).

Nehemiah had a job to do. No one else seemed to notice or care, but he had a vision of his broken city returned to its day of splendor with the rebuilding of its broken walls. Broken cities with broken people, broken walls and broken vows are all around us. And where, pray tell, is God in all of this? Where He always is, of course—waiting for someone to ask of the King and take up the task! Waiting for another to stand in the gap for the city.

Get on the Bus

It all comes down at the end of time to you and those still alive with you at the climax of history.

You stand at a dark and lonely bus stop, waiting for the bus that will take you to your destiny. And a bus pulls up beside you. The door opens, the light comes on, and it waits for you to board.

You look at the front of the bus, just to check to make sure it's the right one. You read the lit sign above the windshield in the darkness, but it's not much help. It just says "CHARTERED."

You think perhaps you'll ask the driver if this is the right bus. After all, it would be an embarrassing, if not terrible thing to get on the wrong bus or one that is not going in the right direction. You look to where the driver is supposed to be seated.

You can't see a driver.

The door is open, the motor is running, but you don't see a driver.

Is this my bus?

Is this the one I'm supposed to take?

Is this the right bus?

Yes. This is the right bus. This is your bus, the one you have been waiting for. It doesn't matter that you don't know right now *where* it is going. It's only important that you know it has been chartered for the journey. It's not even important that you cannot see the driver. Believe me, the bus has a Driver, and He will not fail to deliver you where you must go.

I am afraid.

What if it is the wrong bus?

What if I get on and it takes me someplace I don't want to go?

Maybe I should wait for the next bus.

There *is* no other bus.

This bus comes along only once in a generation, and it only stops once in the place where you stand now.

No one else can ride it for you.

Get on the bus.

SIGNS OF THE TIMES

And I will show wonders in the heavens above and
signs in the earth beneath, blood, and fire, and pillars
[palm trees] of smoke.

Joel 2:30; Acts 2:19
Combined from the *King James Version*

Signs, He said. Signs and wonders in the heavens and earth.
Something unusual marks the generation of the end. A *wonder*—
the Hebrew word *mowpheth* (oddly enough pronounced "mo-
faith")—is an omen, a portent, something that sticks out and
grabs our attention as unusual. A *sign* is, of course, not a destina-
tion; it is simply something symbolic, a marker that points to
something else of real substance and significance. This is indeed
a generation of signs and wonders. There has never been anything like it in all of human history. Look around you. Signs are
everywhere.[1]

THE MARK OF THE PALM TREE

The Japanese anti-aircraft gunners who scrambled in response to
the air-raid siren could not have known. All they saw, if they
could see at all, was a single white parachute high in the sky

above the city of Hiroshima. And if indeed they saw it, it was the last thing they ever looked at. A miniature sun, unnaturally brighter than a thousand flashbulbs, ignited the very air above the city in deadly splendor. All that was left of many of the fleeing people were their shadows burned onto the ruins of the walls.

Mr. Ripley of *Ripley's Believe It or Not*, visiting the terrifying spectacle of the destroyed city in the awful aftermath, could only say, "I am standing on the spot where the end of the world began."

The seventeenth-century *King James* translators, faced with the word *tiymarah* (tee-maw-raw') or *timarah* near the end of Joel 2:30, knew about the pillar of fire by night and the pillar of cloud by day. They knew from the book of Exodus it was a sign of the visitation of God. They knew this word *tiymarah* was not the common word for "pillar," even for the pillar of God's presence. But they went with the simplest translation available. This in translation is always the wisest move, especially when you have no other ready image or model in mind. They knew the root word for what the prophet actually said was *tamar* (taw-ˈmawr) from an unused root meaning "to be erect; standing up like a palm tree." It is only used twice in all the Bible—here and in Song of Solomon 3:6, where the Bride comes out of the wilderness.

Why it would be a sign of the last days of God's visitation was anybody's guess. Any kind of smoke anyone had ever seen went up into the sky either like a pillar or a puff. But a palm tree, with its column trunk and its crown of leaves, looks like both.

They translated it "pillar." *After all, who in the seventeenth century had ever seen smoke that looks like a palm tree?*

THE SIGN OF THE SERVANT

If you buy a Hebrew servant, he shall serve six years; and in the seventh he shall go out free and pay nothing.

But if the servant plainly says, "I love my master, my wife, and my children; I will not go out free," then his master shall bring him to the judges. He shall also bring him to the door, or to the doorpost, and his master shall pierce his ear with an awl; and he shall serve him forever (Exodus 21:2,5,6).

How can someone put up with the pain of a tattoo or a piercing? Tattoos were well known in Jesus' day. Both men and women were marked by their masters much like a cowboy brands cattle—something permanent and painful that forever identified them with the one that ruled them. A Hebrew slave in Bible days who had worked off his six-year debt in the service of his boss was to go free in the seventh year. No Hebrew could legally be a servant of another for longer than that. But sometimes a slave didn't want to leave. Law could no longer hold them, but love might. Hebrew law made provision for such a situation. The master pierced his ear. From then on, much like a wedding ring, the slave's pierced ear was testimony to his voluntary love-slavery to his master.

Many people today put themselves through the pain and permanence that comes with a tattoo, believing it makes them unique. The tattoo is a self-imposed record of bravery: *I faced the pain and made it a permanent part of my life.* In a similar fashion, the ear, nose, nipple, genital or other body part is made the willing target of a body-piercing specialist. When you see someone with a body ring or tattoo, you are supposed to think: *There goes someone who's not afraid to go against the crowd. There goes someone who is both daring and slightly dangerous. There goes someone who has voluntarily faced pain, stared it in the face and now flaunts it for fun.*[2]

Those set apart for God's service in the Old Testament were to be seen as special because of their calling and God's touch on their lives. Only their clothes spoke of their special calling. "They shall neither shave their heads nor let their hair grow long; but they shall keep their hair well trimmed" (Ezekiel 44:20). Idol worshipers marked themselves by the odd way in which they wore their hair or beards or by how they marked their skin. But hair is not the issue. Samson grew his hair long as a sign of his obedience to God (see Numbers 6:5); Paul shaved his head for the same reason (see Acts 21:24-26).

You were made to reflect His glory. Everything you do must honor Him. And despite the slogan of the abortionist, your body is *not* yours. "You are not your own," says Scripture, but "you were bought at a price; therefore glorify God in your body and in your spirit, which are God's" (1 Corinthians 6:19,20). You may already be marked. Yet, from the ranks of those already marked for destruction and death, God will recruit for His purposes to show the world the power of His salvation!

When you see the sign of the pierced ear, watch for the generation that will take the world (Jeff Fenholt, musician, formerly of Black Sabbath).

THE CALL OF THE LAST COMMISSION

So the nations shall fear the name of the Lord,
And all the kings of the earth Your glory.
For the Lord shall build up Zion;
He shall appear in His glory.
He shall regard the prayer of the destitute,
And shall not despise their prayer.
This will be written for the generation to come,
That a people yet to be created may praise the Lord.
For He looked down from the height of His sanctuary;
From heaven the Lord viewed the earth,
To hear the groaning of the prisoner,
To release those appointed to death,

To declare the name of the Lord in Zion,
And His praise in Jerusalem,
When the peoples are gathered together,
And the kingdoms, to serve the Lord (Psalm 102:15-22).

The world at the edge of the New Millennium is marked by explosive growth. Some factors generate figures that form escalating exponential growth charts, not merely linear in form, but functioning at almost incomprehensibly accelerating rates. On such scales, "two" may be ten times greater than "one," and "three" a hundred times greater.

Of all the growth factors that characterize the times in which we live, only a few climb so steeply they need such scales to make them easily measurable. One is the speed of vehicles. One is the power of weaponry. And another is the latest growth of the Christian Church.

Behold, is it not of the Lord of hosts that the peoples labor to feed the fire, and nations weary themselves in vain? For the earth will be filled with the knowledge of the glory of the Lord, as the waters cover the sea (Habakkuk 2:13,14).

These days it seems that must be nothing more than a metaphor, a time when earth is filled with the knowledge of God's glory. But it was this vision that gave the prophets courage to preach to the nations that rejected His truth, reneged on their promises and resisted God's dealings at every turn. How in this time of worldwide darkness and ignorance concerning the beauty and honor of the true Lord of all creation could there ever come a time when people would realize their lives are ugly and empty and begin to acknowledge His right to rule?

Now as He sat on the Mount of Olives, the disciples came to Him privately, saying, "Tell us, when will these things be? And what will be the sign of Your coming, and of the end of the age?"

[And He said] "This gospel of the kingdom will be preached in all the world as a witness to all the nations, and then the end will come" (Matthew 24:3,14).

Even back then people were thinking and talking about the end of all things. Looking at the magnificence of the Temple, over five hundred years of representative history stunningly restored to splendor and a testament to the glory and power that had once been Israel, it was easy for the disciples to think Jesus, too, was probably impressed. But He had cut them short with the shocking word that soon not a single stone of the Temple would be left standing, and His disciples began to think seriously about what it will be like at the end.

When Jesus spoke of the gospel, He talked about a message that was both good news and the announcement of a new order of rulership, a message that His followers were to proclaim as witnesses to all the world. His message was global and inclusive. It would speak to all nations and be preached in all geophysical locations on earth. It was transcultural, touching all of the people groups creating the structures within those nations. It was a message that would prove to be wholly comprehensive; it would speak to them about not just religious matters, but of all things. As E. Stanley Jones said, "If what Jesus said isn't true, it doesn't matter. But if what He said is true, nothing else matters."

"For as the lightning comes from the east and flashes to the west, so also will the coming of the Son of Man be. For wherever the carcass is, there the eagles will be gathered together. Immediately after the tribulation of those days the sun will be darkened, and the moon will not give its light; the stars will fall from heaven, and the powers of the heavens will be shaken.

"Then the sign of the Son of Man will appear in heaven, and then all the tribes of the earth will mourn, and they will see the Son of Man coming on the clouds of heaven with power and great glory. And He will send His angels with a great sound of a trumpet, and they will gather together His elect from the four winds, from one end of heaven to the other" (Matthew 24:27-31).

"When will you restore the Kingdom?" the disciples wanted to know. Like us they were after dates and advance warnings on a calendar. Check the prophecy schedule; if you know when the Master is coming back, you can attempt to get the house cleaned up in time for His homecoming.

We never learn. We still put out the charts and the books and hope things will go badly enough to fit into our schemas for the end of all things. The only thing we can be sure of after reading enough of these is this: Jesus will be back by next Tuesday. And if not, sometime after that.

And He said to them, "It is not for you to know times or seasons which the Father has put in His own authority. But you shall receive power when the Holy Spirit has come upon you; and you shall be witnesses to Me in Jerusalem, and in all Judea and Samaria, and to the end of the earth."

Now when He had spoken these things, while they watched, He was taken up, and a cloud received Him out of their sight.

And while they looked steadfastly toward heaven as He went up, behold, two men stood by them in white apparel, who also said, "Men of Galilee, why do you stand gazing up into heaven? This same Jesus, who was taken

up from you into heaven, will so come in like manner as
you saw Him go into heaven" (Acts 1:7-11).

Jesus didn't give them a calendar; instead He gave them
a commission. He links His return with the accomplishment of a
task given to the Church to carry out in His name and under His
authority with His supernatural equipping. Despite a hesitant
start and the need for much divine encouragement—including
scattering by persecution and repeated clashes with the ruling
religious and political authorities—the Early Church took this
call to heart. Who would have ever thought such a tiny minority
in an obscure corner of the world who followed the words and
leadership of an unknown carpenter from a loser village called
Nazareth could spread under such determined commitment as
to become the largest belief system on earth in the twenty-first
century?

Something is happening before our very eyes that prophets
sought to see from the dawn of God's call to humanity. We may
yet live to see the fulfillment of some of Scripture's greatest
prophecies in all of history. This is the day, indeed, of the dawn-
ing of the Lord.

NOTES
1. All exact meanings of words in languages of the past are inferred, and trans-
    lators do the best they can to convey what they think is the original intent
    of the text in the context of the time. The thing that God said one time
    about one thing may also be fairly and properly applied to a present or
    future thing. Indeed, its very record in sacred writ may be there in the light
    of what is still to come. The statements Jesus made about His betrayal and
    crucifixion (see John 13:18) are actually and literally quotes from King
    David about Ahithophel (see Psalm 41:9) given millennia before by the same
    Spirit that inspired the biblical record. Jesus is not David, but He is the Son
    and the far-descended son of David. Judas is not Ahithophel, but is a betray-
    er nonetheless. Divinely inspired words and phrases used by the prophets
    likewise may convey something more to a modern reader than the prophet
    himself may have realized.
2. The only records of tattoos and other forms of flesh-piercing or cutting in

Scripture are those of men who linked their lives with the occult and devotion to the dead. God takes a very dim view of this (see 1 Kings 18:28; Jeremiah 16:6; Mark 5:5). Demon worshippers practice self-mutilation. It is part of the devil's hatred and jealousy of God's design of our bodies. At the end of time, the Beast seeks to mark the bodies of those that follow him to destruction and torment (see Revelation 13:16,17; 14:9-11; 16:2; 19:20). "They shall not make any bald place on their heads, nor shall they shave the edges of their beards nor make any cuttings in their flesh" (Leviticus 21:5). "You are the children of the Lord your God; you shall not cut yourselves nor shave the front of your head for the dead" (Deuteronomy 14:1).

THE SLACKER GENERATION

For he established a testimony in Jacob, and appointed a law in Israel, which he commanded our fathers, that they should make them known to their children:

That in the last revolution of time, the (slacker) generation to come (from out of the West) might know (by actually seeing) the children (nation, family to come) which shall be born who shall rise to accomplish, (make good, make their mark, celebrate) and declare [them] in turn to their children: That they might set their hope in (the supreme and greatest just) God, and not forget the works of (this Almighty powerful) God, but keep his commandments.

And might not be as their fathers, a stubborn and rebellious generation; a generation that set not their heart aright, (would not stand up at the center for anything) and whose spirit was not steadfast with God. The children of Ephraim, being armed (equipped with weapons), and carrying bows, turned back (became perversely converted back) in the day of battle.

They kept not (did not guard or build a hedge about) the covenant of God and utterly refused to walk in his law. And forgot (became oblivious by not paying attention to) His works, (thoroughly effecting exploits) and His wonders (distinctive marvels & miracles) that He had showed them.

Psalm 78:5-11, *Expanded Hebrew Translation*

The steady rise in social benefits over several decades which parents had come to expect for their children ended with the children of the Baby Boomers. This is the first generation of American children who—based on statistical projections—know that things will not be better for them than for those who came before them. They arrived too late to reap the benefits of the post-World War II economic expansion, inheriting a bankrupt system in which there are no longer jobs for life, giant holes in the social safety nets for those that cannot make it and reduced help from government welfare.

Most of the lost tribes at the edge of the New Millennium have a built-in resistance to big schemes and big dreams, because they face the prospect of a world that offers little realistic hope. Parents who grew up in a time when drive, ambition and "get-up-and-go" were held as ideals cannot handle their children's *laissez-faire* attitudes. The media have bestowed upon them a name that sums up their always-late, left-out, left-behind, slow-to-get-there spirit.

They call them Slackers.

Psalm 78 speaks of a "generation to come" and reveals the background to their birth. It speaks of God's dealings with their parents before them, of a great divine visitation marked by wonders and miracles. The visitation was not just for blessing; it was to give them courage and faith for a great battle to come upon them in the near future.

These parents were given both short-range and long-range weaponry to prepare them for the battle at hand and a greater one still beyond that. Yet on the very eve of the battle, just when it counted most, they forgot their covenant with God, forgot what He had done and what He said, forgot both His works and His wonders. They abandoned their call, folded their tents and their hearts and left their children to face the war alone.

There have been many generations in history that might claim for themselves the promise in this passage, who likewise found themselves in the situation described in Psalm 78. You are not the only ones in history that might claim it, but you most certainly fit the spirit and intention of God's protective visitation.[1]

While historical records in Scripture are rarely subject to interpretation, prophetic phrases certainly are, as we try to determine from a past declaration a future intention of God. This is tricky in an original language, let alone in a translation. God speaks to people about what He intends to do beyond what they can possibly see, and we know that because of the nature of such revelation, prophets often recorded what they did not understand.

Who are the people described in this prophetic psalm? They are simply called "the generation to come." The phrase is not common, only used this way twice in the Bible. The word "generation" means a revolution of time, another whole cycle of history.

The root word *achar*, from which the phrase *acharon* is derived, is even more interesting. Used sixteen times in the Bible, it is variously translated and used in negative terms, meaning to hinder, hold back, defer, put off, be slow in coming, to tarry.[2] It is used to describe this particular culture of hindered, last, late and left-behind young people. One of the scriptural ways it is translated, "slack," happens to be the very epithet given GenXers—Slackers—in exactly the same situation the passage describes.

The actual phrase "to come" (late or last—*acharon*) used here is translated from the root word *achar*, and it is the most fascinating of all. According to *Strong's*, it literally means *facing the East*, i.e. *Western*. While in the original context of this verse it certainly meant something significant to the generation who first heard it, in the light of world missionary activity where the Holy Spirit forbade Paul and Silas to go toward the East and head toward the West instead (see Acts 16:6-10), it is even more significant.

As we trace the chain of Christianity in historical missions, the work of the Spirit begins in the West and looks now as if it will finish in the East. Asia, the cradle of human civilization, is where the human race began. Many Bible scholars believe that the regions of Babylon and Persia, power centers of the great demonic principalities of Scripture and now called Iran and Iraq, may have been the geographic location of the Garden of Eden.

Sin came to the garden and spread outward from the East to the West. *In world missions, God is taking His world back again in reverse.* The last great staging area is the East. China is presently experiencing the greatest awakening in world history with some 28,000 people a day coming to Christ.

In the purposes and destiny of God, it is toward this last great mission field of the Unfinished Task that the present GenXers and GenNexters out of the West are pointed now.

NOTES

1. A good guide for life is that "all the promises of God in [Christ] are Yes, and in Him Amen, to the glory of God through us" (2 Corinthians 1:20). Everything God does is done in perfect justice, integrity and faithfulness. He commands without partiality or prejudice, and never makes His promises randomly (see 1 Timothy 5:21; James 3:17). If we find ourselves in the situation of any promise made to any of God's people in Scripture and are able and willing to meet the explicit or implicit conditions of those promises, God may also in His grace and mercy fulfill that promise for us. Jesus is "the same yesterday, today, and forever" (Hebrews 13:8). Any promise made to anyone in the Bible may be fulfilled in Christ.

2. For instance, *achar* is used when the mother of the evil Sisera looked out at a window, and "cried through the lattice, Why is his chariot so long in coming? Why [tarry] the wheels of his chariot?" (Judges 5:28, *KJV*). "Those who [tarry] long at the wine" (Proverbs 23:30). "Woe to those who rise early in the morning, that they may follow intoxicating drink; who [continue] until night, till wine inflames them!" (Isaiah 5:11). "It is vain for you to rise up early, to sit up [late], to eat the bread of sorrows; for so He gives His beloved sleep" (Psalm 127:2). The word is used negatively to show God "will not be [slack] with him who hates Him; He will repay him to his face" (Deuteronomy 7:10) and that "when you make a vow to God, do not [delay] to pay it; for He has no pleasure in fools. Pay what you have vowed" (Ecclesiastes 5:4).

PART IV

MARKS OF THE MILLENNIALISTS: WHAT MAKES THIS GENERATION DIFFERENT?

SURVIVORS:
DEATH, DIVORCE AND
WHATEVER

You shall not worship the Lord your God in that way;
for every abomination to the Lord which He hates
they have done to their gods; for they burn even their
sons and daughters in the fire to their gods.

Deuteronomy 12:31

There is nothing more *unnatural* in the world than for a mother
to murder her own child. The worshipers of Baal and Molech
who offered the chosen of their children to idols were not primi-
tives; they were citizens of a civilization that was one of the most
advanced of its time. To understand the horror of what happened, imagine a society of Silicon Valley executives who meet
every Sunday at 11:00 A.M. to worship and pray with devotional
music played loudly enough to drown out the screams of their
own children as they are burned to death on an altar.[1]

The terror of the moment in America is the once unthinkable
spectacle of children killing children. In small towns across the
nation, children are becoming mass murderers, *unnatural born
killers*. We profess to be shocked, but why should we be? Children
die every day, the innocent victims of terrorism, gang warfare,

malnutrition, abortion. But few notice any more; we have become accustomed to the holocaust. The pro-choice parental predator has become politically correct.

Baal and Molech never went away. Only their names have been changed so as *not* to protect the innocent. Idol worship goes on today in a world that sacrifices its future inheritance to pleasure, property and power in the name of convenience and freedom. The valley of Hinnom, the original site of those terrible child sacrifices, eventually came to be called Gehenna. A garbage dump on the edge of the city, Gehenna is one of the Bible's names for *hell*.

Unthinkable for God: Child Sacrifice

"And they built the high places of Baal which are in the Valley of the Son of Hinnom, to cause their sons and their daughters to pass through the fire to Molech, which I did not command them, *nor did it come into My mind* that they should do this abomination, to cause Judah to sin" (Jeremiah 32:35).

Some things our society does are beyond belief, even for heaven. The cult of child sacrifice for money, power and luxury is something not even omniscience entertains as a possibility, but we make laws to protect our right to do it.

We worship three "good" gods in the West: education, status and money. Churchgoing people, who will otherwise live exemplary lives before the watching world, are still willing to sacrifice their children to these ancient pretenders to the throne.

"Let not the wise man glory in his wisdom, let not the mighty man glory in his might, nor let the rich man glory in his riches; but let him who glories glory in this, that he understands and knows Me, that I am the Lord" (Jeremiah 9:23,24).

God is the wealthiest Being in the Universe. He likes gold; He thinks it makes nice paving material. God is the smartest Person in the Universe. He didn't need to call anyone into consultation when He built the worlds with but a word. God is the most powerful, wonderful, influential Ruler of all time. One day every knee will bow and every tongue confess that He is who He really declares Himself to be. So what should we seek first in our lives? Practically speaking, can we seriously believe the most important things in life are to be rich, smart and famous?

There was a respected deacon in a great evangelical church, a man who had lived a life of integrity and honor and was known as a man who upheld biblical truth in his life. In keeping with his reputation for excellence in everything he did, he urged his children to excel in fields where they would likewise be known and respected in the community, and he took every opportunity to equip and prepare them to be leaders of their professions. And they did, indeed, become the leaders he had primed them to be. But he wept near the end of his life as he watched them—all smart, wealthy and influential professionals—walk away from God and spend their careers serving themselves. We become like the gods we worship.

REVERSAL: THE DARK LINK TO CHILD DEATH

And he caused his children to pass through the fire in the valley of the son of Hinnom: also he observed times, and used enchantments, and used witchcraft, and dealt with a familiar spirit, and with wizards: he wrought much evil

in the sight of the Lord, to provoke him to anger
(2 Chronicles 33:6, *KJV*).

What is it about a child that draws such interest from the occult
world? The core of satanic strategy is always about *reversal*—going
against the normal, the natural, the loveliness of the ordinary.
G. K. Chesterton saw it. When in *The Everlasting Man* the devil
worshiper carved the terrible face of his idol in the dark red wood
of the forest, he was making a bargain with hell. In setting out
against all that was beautiful, all that was created normal and
alive, he was aiming to tap the very fount out of which the power
to make all things had flowed. He hoped he could carve an image
at whose sight the very sky would crack like a mirror and open to
him the foundations of the universe.[2]

Reversal is hell's power-play for the Creation of God. A child
is a gift from God, the epitome of new life, the beginning of all
human possibility. Little children are illustrations of God's idea
of the kingdom of heaven. Where children are dying unnaturally,
look for the activity of demons.

He went to a little country school, a fifteen-year-old fresh-
man. He was the unwanted child of parents with unhappy
multiple marriages on both sides of the family. One day he called
a friend and told him he was going to finish it all. That Sunday
night he went into his mother's bedroom, slashed her throat,
stabbed her again and again and then put a bullet through his
own brain.

Somehow his mother survived. She said later it was probably
the drugs and the bad friends that had made him crazy. At his sister's request, they played Marilyn Manson at his funeral.

In the aftermath of his suicide something happened to one of
the young man's friends. A Christian teenager who was witnessing to him went over to his house for a martial arts workout, and
during the course of that brief time felt led to share with the
friend a vivid visual impression God had given him of heaven.

The day before the funeral, a coach at the high school asked in a school assembly if anyone wanted to say anything about the dead boy. That morning the Lord had spoken to the Christian boy about witnessing: "I am come that they might have life and have it more abundantly. Go. Tell them of My undying love."

He stood up that day and told his school, "He was my friend, but he killed himself. I believe there is a real hell and a real heaven. I believe he was in pain. He was hurting and he had no way to stop the pain. He took drugs and he killed himself. I know why you take drugs. It's not to be cool or to fit in or to be respected. It's because you're in pain and it's a way to numb the pain. Don't die like he did. Don't die and go to hell. Jesus came that you might have life. He didn't know Jesus. And I don't want any of you to die without knowing Jesus."

A few of his other friends stood up after him. They too came forward to remember the boy who hurt so much and felt so unwanted that he couldn't live with himself anymore. "No one paid attention to him," they said. "No one cared. But we cared about him. He was our friend." They talked about what school did to people like that. He went unnoticed in school, but when he killed himself, the whole school noticed. They acknowledged that what the Christian boy had said was true.

Afterward one of them told the Christian, "We had a suicide pact together. When I knew he'd done it, I was going to kill myself too. But then you told me about heaven, and I couldn't get that picture of heaven out of my mind."

CLEANSING FIRE, HOLY DESTRUCTION: DEFILING THE SITES OF DEMONS

And he defiled Topheth, which is in the Valley of the Son of Hinnom, that no man might make his son or his daughter pass through the fire to Molech (2 Kings 23:10).

And if a stranger dwells with you, or whoever is among
you throughout your generations, and would present an
offering made by fire, a sweet aroma to the Lord, just as
you do, so shall he do (Numbers 15:14).

Defiling Topheth and kindling a new fire. Something must be done to
stop false worship in a way that will make a lasting impression on
those who practice idolatry. It has happened before in history.

They were sometimes only twelve years old. All they had to do
was to take a single sip of the offered wine to acknowledge to the
assembled crowds that the watching emperor was a god and
the rightful ruler of the world. Around them were the crosses or
the stakes on which many of their parents and relatives would die
that day, some whose heads were dipped in pitch and set on fire
as grisly torches to light the arena for the games. A single sip and
they need not face the wild animals that had been starved
and goaded and tortured in preparation to face helpless
Christians in the arena in front of the people of Rome.

A single sip. *But they would not do it.* Yes, they were afraid. They
sometimes wept and they all prayed, but they would not deny
Christ. One said, "These lions are not our enemies but our
friends. They will usher us into the arms of Jesus." And it was said
that for every Christian who died in the jaws of the lions, seven
Romans watching became Christians. Thus the Early Church
grew.

There is something that often goes unnoticed when the story
is told of the plagues that hit Egypt during Moses' confrontation
with the most powerful world leader of his day. Each one of
the plagues was set against a representation of deity worshiped by
the Egyptians. They worshiped the image of a frog, and the land
was filled with them. They worshiped the river Nile as the giver of
life, and it turned to blood in their hands. The priests kept their
heads shaven so as to remain perfectly free from the contamina-
tion of any head infestation. As Moses touched the dust of the

ground, the lice that multiplied guaranteed no worship would be offered to a demonic deity in Egypt that day.

The judgement of God always shows up what is held as idolatrously sacred, special and significant. His judgement unmasks the idol, revealing it as merely polluted, filthy and small. The demonic can duplicate many miracles in its own magic version of lying wonders, but it is proved powerless to create even the tiniest new life. The lord of the flies has no equal footing with the Lord of heaven, and we should learn this quickly if we are to avoid another visit from a messenger like Moses out of the desert. Life always triumphs over death in the end, but sometimes the confirming evidence comes at a terrible cost.

Duels to the death as Roman spectacle thrived until one day the Christian monk Telemachus jumped into the arena and stood between the warring gladiators with his agonized appeal: "In the name of Jesus Christ, stop this!"

Telemachus died that day, but so did the duels. So many were sickened by the sight of that loving self-sacrifice that it cut the hating heart out of the callous crowd. Never again were the Romans able to hold gladiator contests in the arenas. Thus ended a perverted display of deaths that had gone on for decades. Telemachus defiled Topheth for good.

He was not the last person who would do like Jesus did and interpose his own life between the consequences of sin and the future. Today, we cannot die like Jesus, but we can live and love like Him.

Moses did this when he stood in the gap between the just judgement of an outraged God and the fate of his nation, when he prayed, "If you will not forgive my people's sin, then blot me out of Your book which You have written" (see Exodus 32:30-33).

Paul did the same when he said, "I tell the truth in Christ, I am not lying, my conscience also bearing me witness in the Holy Spirit, that I have great sorrow and continual grief in my heart. For I could wish that I myself were accursed from Christ for my brethren, my countrymen according to the flesh" (Romans 9:1-3). Men willing to go to hell for others are rare.

Not all defiling of Topheths involve such self-sacrificial demonstration. Yet God always manages to find those who will show such deep love for Him and for their fellow humans. The motto of the Moravian missionaries stood for a century, as they even sold themselves into slavery to win the slaves and became themselves lepers in leper colonies to win the lepers: "To win for the Lamb that was slain the reward of their suffering."

And the cleansing fire that such as these kindled still burns through the world as a witness.

There's Always a Hidden Deliverer

And there appeared a great wonder in heaven; a woman clothed with the sun, and the moon under her feet, and upon her head a crown of twelve stars: And she being with child cried, travailing in birth, and pained to be delivered. And there appeared another wonder in heaven; and behold a great red dragon . . . and the dragon stood before the woman which was ready to be delivered, for to devour her child as soon as it was born. And she brought forth a man child, who was to rule all nations with a rod of iron: and her child was caught up unto God, and to his throne (Revelation 12:1-5, *KJV*).

At least three times, at critical moments in history, the world has declared war on the children. Tradition holds that this was true in the time of Abraham. The Bible tells us this was true in the time of Moses and again in the days of Jesus' birth. There seems to be some kind of hellish signal that goes out into the darkness: "A deliverer is coming! Gates will fall and massive losses will be incurred at the hands of the righteous." So a contract is put out to spill the blood of the children of that critical time.

Death walks once again. The cry of the bereaved goes up to heaven as the innocent casualties mount, fueling the fires of a generation's destruction. Hell sometimes seems to know better than the Church the critical nature of the hour. Yet in every case, heaven's own promised deliverer has escaped the sword and the flame and lived to visit the vengeance of God on the enemies of life and love and destiny.

In our time, that war has come again.

One-third of your generation never even made it out of the womb. Sixteen million in America alone fell victim to abortion, never given a chance to make any kind of a mark in a world they never saw.[3] Of those who lived, half have had to somehow survive the disintegration of their families, the bitter breaking of marriage bonds meant to shelter and sustain them. They were turned out into the world without the inner moorings necessary to deal with perhaps the most deadly culture in history.

You are survivors of a siege against divine destiny. As before, hidden somewhere among you is a promised child that has escaped the dragon. Only this time, there's not just one, but many. And they will take the battle to the end of the world.

NOTES

1. Winkie Pratney, *Devil Take the Youngest* (Lafayette, LA: Huntingdon House, 1985), pp. 74-82.
2. G. K. Chesterton, "The War of the Gods and the Demons," *The Everlasting Man* (Costa Mesa, CA: PMA/Dodd-Mead, 1943).
3. Abortion, like all other sins, can be forgiven, and the grace of God can bring real pardon and peace to parents who took the life of an unborn child. It is significant that even in *Roe vs. Wade*, the test case used to legally justify abortion, the mother became a Christian and is now herself publicly speaking out against this sin and sharing about God's forgiveness to others.

ORPHANS
OR
FREEDOM'S JUST ANOTHER WORD FOR NOTHING LEFT TO LOSE

And it came to pass, when David and his men were
come to Ziklag on the third day, that the Amalekites
had invaded the south, and Ziklag, and smitten
Ziklag, and burned it with fire. So David and his men
came to the city, and, behold, it was burned with fire;
and their wives, and their sons,
and their daughters, were taken captives.
Then David and the people who were with him lifted
up their voice and wept,
until they had no more power to weep.

1 Samuel 30:1,2,4, *KJV*

Our holy and beautiful temple, where our fathers
praised You, is burned up with fire; and all
our pleasant things are laid waste

Isaiah 64:11

Terrible loss brings us quickly and intimately in touch with reality. The hippie counterculture of the '60s and '70s failed finally to rewire the consciousness of a generation because they missed out on the one ingredient they most needed: They knew how to sing, how to dance and how to laugh, but they didn't know how to *cry*. They went to the streets to learn how to love, but never had the power to truly weep for one another. GenX faces the same challenge. They already know the hurt, the loss, the pain. What is needed now is a baptism of tears.

REAPING FROM THE RANKS OF THE REJECTED

It is instructive to note how many people in the Bible mightily used by God were orphaned or in some way rejected, despised or abandoned early in their lives by their real parents.[1]

Joseph was hated by his brothers and sold into slavery but would later rise to power in a strange land and save his brothers' lives during the great famine.

Moses was adopted by Pharaoh's daughter and raised as a prince but would be forever remembered, not as one of a long line Pharaohs, but as God's chosen deliverer who led a nation out of bondage.

Daniel, Shadrach, Meshach and Abed-Nego were orphaned and alienated from their homes and marched off into captivity in Babylon, yet they wound up ruling the world under the kings who had captured them.

Jeptha, son of a harlot and thrown out of his father's house by his "proper" sons, stood in the gap and fought for his nation against the enemy, the only one who could do it.

Esther the beauty queen was adopted by her uncle and later saved her nation.

Ruth was widowed young but would remarry, bear a son and

become an earthly ancestor of King David and, eventually, Jesus Christ.

God has a special thing for orphaned and abandoned people.

He administers justice for the fatherless and the widow, and loves the stranger, giving him food and clothing (Deuteronomy 10:18).

"Leave your fatherless children, I will preserve them alive; and let your widows trust in Me" (Jeremiah 49:11).

Elizabeth Moberley points out that much of what we call "gay" or "lesbian" in our culture is often the sad result of children being virtually orphaned and abandoned by parents of the same sex. Their deep hunger and need for early same-sex love is turned (in our sensual society) to sexual ends. The children grow up driven in a wrong direction, abandoned by the very ones who should have loved and cared and sheltered them when they were small. Sin must be repented of, but needs must be met.

There will be a great reaping from the ranks of the rejected when the revelation of the Father's heart for orphans is seen and understood by a hurting, orphaned generation.[2]

DAVID'S FAMILY SECRET

Who was David? Everyone knows him as the musical genius who wrote most of the Psalms, songs we still sing today after 3,000 years. Everyone knows he was the one who brought down the God-defying Goliath of Gath, the ten-feet-tall Philistine mutant with a spear as big as a telegraph pole and an attitude to match. Everyone knows David became Israel's greatest ruler, the most beloved king Israel ever had. In God's own words, he was a man after God's own heart (see 1 Samuel 13:14).

Yet there are some mysteries about David and his family. Scripture says Jesse had seven sons, and it also says he had eight. David was apparently the youngest, and while the youngest in a family usually gets treated well by everyone, in David's case this does not seem to be true at all. And David is so different from the others!

What is hard to understand is why his brothers all seemed to hate him, and why his dad hid him up in the hills when Samuel came to anoint one of Jesse's sons to be Israel's future king (see 1 Samuel 16). Even Samuel was fooled looking at Eliab, the oldest and coolest, when the prophet came up to him at the head of the line with the anointing oil in his hand. Yet none of the seven sons in the line had the call of God. Samuel asks Jesse, "Do you have any other sons besides these?" Embarrassed, Jesse said he had left David behind. After all, someone had to take care of the sheep! Yet when David is sent down to bring his brothers food during Israel's war with the Philistines, they obviously had somebody to take care of the sheep *then* (see 1 Samuel 17:20).

David did not just have brothers; he also had two sisters, Zeruiah and Abigail (see 1 Chronicles 2:16). His sister Zeruiah had three sons: Joab, Abishai and Asahel (see 1 Samuel 26:6; 2 Samuel 2:18), at least one of whom figured prominently in David's military campaigns. What is odd is that when David's lineage is given in Scripture, his sisters' dad's name is not Jesse, but Nahash! (See 2 Samuel 17:25.) David's father is, of course, Jesse. We are not told the name of David's mother.

Question: How is David related to his sisters if both he and his sisters have different fathers? Answer: *Only if they have the same mother.* And if they do, she is not the wife of Jesse but of Nahash.

There are, of course, other possible explanations. Perhaps Jesse was also known as Nahash, though this is unlikely. Or perhaps Jesse may have married a woman who was formerly married to Nahash. Is it possible that Jesse lost his first wife and remarried and David was the only son of that later marriage? David's two sisters did have children of around his own age. But for this to be true, Nahash also would have had to have died after begetting David's two sisters, and his wife quickly remarried to Jesse.

There is an even simpler and more embarrassing possibility not mentioned by most commentaries: *David's mother was not Jesse's wife.* Jesse was not married to David's mother when she conceived him. If this is so, it would explain a lot about David's rejection by his brothers and the seeming embarrassment of his family.

Of course, there are no illegitimate children, only adults involved in illegitimate affairs. David was not to blame for his situation, whatever it may have been. But an "illegitimate" birth would explain the strange attitude of his older brothers when he appeared at the battlefield and his exclusion from the line-up when Samuel came to anoint one of Jesse's sons to be king.

If this is indeed the case, as some Jewish commentators believe, if David was the product of a secret affair of his father with Nahash's wife, then he would have been considered a shame to his family and kept out of the public eye as much as possible. David was the one who said, "When my father and my mother forsake me, then the Lord will take care of me" (Psalm 27:10) and "In sin my mother conceived me"[3] (Psalm 51:5).

Under these circumstances, David could have become bitter. He could have grown into an angry, rejected young man, full of hurt and hatred. Instead he took his lonely heart to the God he called "Father" and sang his songs to Him up in the hills with his sheep and his lyre. And the God of all justice, the God who loves orphans, whose eyes run to and fro throughout the whole earth, made David the greatest king Israel ever had.

A WALL OF FIRE: BLOWING UP
BRIDGES TO THE PAST

He put a wall of fire around me,
He put a fence between my soul and the Enemy.
Satan's power can't penetrate
The wall that Jesus' love creates.
He put a wall of fire around me.
(Song of a new Christian rescued from witchcraft during
the Jesus Movement)

When Solomon had finished praying, fire came down
from heaven, and consumed the burnt offering and the
sacrifices; and the glory of the Lord filled the temple. And
the priests could not enter the house of the Lord, because
the glory of the Lord had filled the Lord's house. When
all the children of Israel saw how the fire came down, and
the glory of the Lord on the temple, they bowed their
faces to the ground on the pavement, and worshiped and
praised the Lord, saying: "For He is good, for His mercy
endures forever" (2 Chronicles 7:1-3).

Sometimes during a rally or crusade I will call for a Day of
Destruction. On one night, kids can bring to the altar something
that represents to them the heart and essence of what they must
give up to demonstrate they mean business in getting wholly
right with God.

I teach them that true repentance means that we will *see, hate*
and *forsake* our sin; if we are to break from what we have loved to
the point of addiction, we must see it and hate it like God sees it
and hates it. They then publicly destroy that thing that has hurt
them in the most violent way they can. In the front we often have

large metal garbage cans. The kids will destroy on their own the items they have brought, or get a little help from their friends, and then abandon the remains in these trash cans. Then we set them on fire.

Kids bring all kinds of things to a destruction rally—demonic gods, dirty gods, once-precious gods, even "good" gods that have simply gotten in the way of the one true God. Sometimes other kids will join in to help someone break or shatter or tear that representative god beyond repair as a radical demonstration of an utter break with the past. Ushers have seen all kinds of things thrown into those cans—magazines, videos, CDs, tapes, books, clothes, money, credit cards, jewelry.

"For I," says the Lord, "will be a wall of fire all around her, and I will be the glory in her midst" (Zechariah 2:5).

One beautifully dressed young woman walked to the front and dropped a pair of expensive black patent-leather high-heeled shoes into the garbage can. Catching the eye of the puzzled usher posted near the trash can, she said simply, "You don't know what this means and nobody else in here knows what this means, but I know what it means and God knows what it means." Around that single action I could probably make a whole movie that started off with just that pair of shoes and what they stood for and meant to her that night and for the rest of her life.

Item: It comes right at the end of a three-day worship conference. The final session is nearly eight hours of unashamed praise and honor to God, involving some of the best Christian worship leaders on the planet. The conference leader then asks one of the worship leaders to sing a highly unusual song—a modified version of one of the early Beatles' most famous tunes, "I Wanna Hold Your Hand," released not too long before John Lennon stated in a notorious interview that the Beatles were more popular than Jesus Christ. Only this time the song is sung as if Christ the Bridegroom is singing to His Beloved, the Church. The sense of the presence of God intensifies to an even greater level at the end of the song, as wave after wave of worship erupts in the building.

Then something begins to happen on stage. There is a scent of rare perfume in the air. One of the worship singers begins to feel as if her clothes are on fire; another goes to her face on the floor behind the instruments. The sense of the presence of God is so strong no one can stand anymore.

Later, as they replay the tapes, they will hear a sound like wind in the microphones moving around the building, but no one notices at the time. The whole of their attention is riveted on what they see happening before their very eyes. As the whole congregation hushes in awed silence, *a cloud appears on stage.* It remains there long enough for everyone to see it, then moves away and vanishes as one of the worship singers sings a song of devotional longing to Christ. Later, the leader announces, "Tonight, we're taking something back."[4]

NOTES

1. There are seven categories of hurting people God promises special help to in Scripture—the stranger, the poor, the oppressed, the innocent, the hired servant, the widow and the orphaned of His people: "Thus says the Lord: Execute judgment and righteousness, and deliver the plundered out of the hand of the oppressor: Do no wrong and do no violence to the stranger, the fatherless, or the widow, nor shed innocent blood in this place" (Jeremiah 22:3). "Learn to do well; seek judgment, relieve the oppressed, judge the fatherless, plead for the widow" (Isaiah 1:17, *KJV*). This is why ministries like Adopt-a-Block and Somebody Cares are so effective.

   God promises to deal hard with those in authority who abuse their power to further hurt those with no power to resist. "Your princes are rebellious, and companions of thieves; everyone loves bribes, and follows after rewards. They do not defend the fatherless, nor does the cause of the widow come before them" (Isaiah 1:23). "To turn aside the needy from judgment, and to take away the right from the poor of my people, that widows may be their prey, and that they may rob the fatherless!" (Isaiah 10:2, *KJV*). "And I will come near you for judgment; I will be a swift witness against sorcerers, against adulterers, against perjurers, against those who exploit wage earners and widows and orphans, and against those who turn away an alien—because they do not fear Me," says the Lord of hosts (Malachi 3:5).

2. Elizabeth R. Moberley, *Homosexuality: A New Ethic* (Cambridge, England: James Clarke & Co. Ltd.). See my summary of her work on the implications for ministry to gays in "God's Care for Orphans," *The Nature and Character of God* (Minneapolis: Bethany, 1988), pp. 341-343.

3. It is significant to note that the subject of the last verse here is David's mother. He is not saying, as in some translations, that he was born sinful but that his mother's act of his own conception was sin.

4. "Restoring Worship to Its Proper Owner," the *Glory* CD from the Heart of David worship conference, 1998.

WORSHIPERS: CONVICTIONS, COMMITMENT AND ABANDONMENT

Set me as a seal upon your heart, as a seal upon
your arm; for love is as strong as death, jealousy
as cruel as the grave; its flames are flames
of fire, a most vehement flame.

Song of Solomon 8:6

Who makes His angels spirits,
His ministers a flame of fire.

Psalm 104:4

So I turned and came down from the mountain, and
the mountain burned with fire; and the two tablets of
the covenant were in my two hands.

Deuteronomy 9:15

There is one thing you'll never have to teach this generation, and
that is the *power of worship*. Unlike previous pretenders to the
throne, they understand that something you give your life over to

is worth an utter abandonment. Nothing will be permitted to come between them and the object of their devotion.

One thing GenX and GenNexter tribes have in common is commitment to their music. Music is at the core of many kids' lives. It does far more than serve as background for driving, homework or partying; it pragmatically defines cultural boundaries. The music you like tells others which tribe you belong to. Touch the music of GenX and GenNexter tribes and you touch the real focus of their worship.

Frank Zappa said decades ago, "The only real loyalty that exists today for a teenager is his music. He doesn't give an actual damn about his country, his mother, his government or his religion." Visit a concert and see how close kids get to the object of their affection. You never have to coach them to "give it up" or to "give it all." They already know what real worship is. They just don't know who to give that gift to.

CHART-MAKERS AND THE ABILITY TO EXPRESS CONVICTION

What makes a core chart-maker, that rare recording artist who could perform the phone book and take it to number one on the Top 40? Define that and you could write your own ticket in New York, Nashville or Hollywood. There are myriads of possibilities and factors that make the difference between a no-name garage band, a one-hit wonder and an enduring superstar, not the least of which is talent. But some artists seem to stick in the sensibility of a culture and become icons forever. And one thing they have in common above all others appears essential to contemporary endurance: the ability to communicate *conviction* to an audience.

Elvis, the Beatles, the Stones, Springsteen, U2, Madonna, Garth Brooks. It doesn't matter what the conviction is, but it must be real and it must show. Lose your convictions for this crowd and you lose your listeners. Prove you are not really the person you claim to be and whether you are Milli Vanilli or Michael Jackson, your audience will abandon you.

> Make my life a prayer to You.
> I want to do what You want me to.
> No empty words and no white lies,
> No token prayers, no compromise.
>
> — Keith Green

Times have changed in the Church too. Though not all agree on what music is of God and what is not, and while many Christian music companies have been co-opted by big-money marketing labels, and though the temptations of wealth, status and pleasure are as alive to the Christian artist as to his secular counterpart, music still speaks and sings its prophetic song to the saints. And every now and then the notes get through with conviction. It is significant that the most popular Christian music in the world is contemporary worship. We've come a long way from "Kum Ba Yah."

When Moses came down from the mountain that burned with fire, holding the law of God fresh from the hand of God, the first thing that greeted him was the sound of a rival worship (see Exodus 32:17-19). The drunken orgy around the golden cow at the foot of Jabal el Lawz was a direct attempt to hijack the one thing man can truly give to God that is his own: his worship. Times have not changed. Look around you. Cows and parties are springing up everywhere.

Of course our objects of worship look a little different. We worship not only musicians and movie stars but sports figures too. We will give international attention to an athlete or athletic event no one could ever imagine would draw a crowd for something *religious*. Yet I am inclined to believe that God is able to speak and does so in areas and arenas where we least expect to hear His voice.

BULLY PULPIT: TYSON VS. HOLYFIELD

Without doubt the most astonishing boxing match of the century had to be the first fight between Mike Tyson and Evander Holyfield. One man was known as the most dangerous boxer of his time, crushing bodies and faces with a focused rage that left few standing in its wake; the other an aging world champion most said didn't have a prayer.

After all, Evander Holyfield had a hole in his heart. It had knocked him out of boxing, indeed should have knocked him out of *everything*. Yet at a healing crusade he attended, the evangelist not only prayed for his heart, but he also had a prophetic word for Holyfield's career and his family: *Go back to the ring. You must make money to take care of your wife and children.* Later, tests from the Mayo Clinic showed that not only was there no sign of heart damage, but that Holyfield was in absolutely perfect health. This is now known to the world as the "misdiagnosed heart condition."

The difference between the Tyson and Holyfield training camps was entire and extreme. In one, the Islamic brotherhood urged on their fighter for the glory of Allah, to show to the world his power and force; in the other, a man learned to worship Christ in a workout. In one camp, multiple training partners provided a diverse and varied attack for the challenger; in the other, there stood a single Christian friend, David Tua of New Zealand, another champion who unashamedly witnessed for Christ.

In the Holyfield locker room before the fight, to a man praying with his wife before the most challenging confrontation of his entire career, the comparison to David and Goliath was obvious. "Maybe you should do what David did," Holyfield's wife suggested. "He danced before the Lord."

"How do you do that?"

"I don't know. Perhaps just sing to Him and move in time to it."

In the other locker room they were punching lockers and yelling; in this one, a man was dancing and singing a hymn.

Everyone now knows the details of the unbelievable events of that night. They told Holyfield to stay away; he moved in. They told him to defend himself; he took the attack right to the man known as Iron Mike. For those who are into the biblical significance of numbers, in the sixth round—six being the number of man under sin—Tyson, already losing on points, went on his rear end to the canvas. By the eleventh round—eleven being the number of disorganization—Tyson didn't know where he was anymore, and the referee stopped the fight.

Afterwards, Holyfield, to the embarrassment of the Las Vegas crowd, witnessed to the watching world—the largest in the history of boxing—of the power of Christ. When asked about his strategy for the fight the champion said, "I asked the Holy Spirit to show me round by round."

The contrast between the two fighters in the short, stupefying sequel was even more amazing—one fighter coming into the ring to the sound of gangsta rap, the other to the strains of a worship chorus: "When the Spirit of the Lord moves in my heart, I will pray like David prayed."

God doesn't just speak at evangelistic meetings or from pulpits on Sunday. Sometimes He uses the things that men respect and hear in the very world where you would least expect to hear Him speak. It doesn't spoil the magic to learn that the men God may use to speak to others can still themselves be deeply flawed and further in need of the ministry of the Savior. And for those of you who do not believe God can speak through the world of sports, remember that three sports are mentioned in the New

Testament as illustrations of winning in the Christian life—running a race, wrestling an opponent and boxing another contender without beating the air.

LONG-DISTANCE LOVE:
THE WAY OF MODERN SAINTHOOD

We don't need another hero.

— Tina Turner

Who do you look up to in a culture like ours? Who do you trust? Who do you model your life after? Who do you want to be like?

Your god, after all, is the person or thing that means the most to you in life. It is the thing you like to talk about most, the thing your thoughts turn back to when you have nothing better to do, the person or thing your life actually revolves around, the thing you spend most of your money on, the one thing you would rather die than live without. That—whatever else you may say—is your real god, the actual deity of your devotion.

Our heroes tend to be cartoon characters, musicians and movie stars who exist only in the media. The people we want to be like are rich, famous, strong, good-looking and have the morals of an alley cat. Think for a moment about the recent deaths of two well-known women. One was pretty, young, fabulously wealthy and graced the cover of every major magazine in the world. The other was wrinkled, plain, poor and old. She spent her life loving the sick and the dying. One prominent church leader, watching her hug a diseased and dying child, said to her, "I wouldn't do that for a hundred thousand dollars."

"Neither would I," she said. "I do it for Jesus."

When Diana, the young woman with the goddess name, died,

the whole world mourned. They sang songs about her, heaped millions of flowers along the roads at her funeral and wept as if she were a member of their own families. They apparently did not remember that this girl, who might once have inherited the role and responsibility of guardianship of the Church in her nation and still was in charge of the spiritual futures of her royal sons, the rightful heirs to the throne, died tragically after a series of immoral affairs. They knew she was a desperately unhappy, lonely divorcée struggling with bulimia; they identified with her struggles to make a better life for herself. But they apparently forgot that she died right after consulting a psychic medium and that she was seriously involved with a Muslim playboy who might have brought her children—heirs to the throne—into the Islamic faith.

The world wept as if she were their own because, in a very real way, she was. Diana was the epitome of all we hold wonderful in our time. Diana was the fairy-tale princess with the storybook wedding and a tragic tabloid marriage—the wounded survivor on a quest for what we think of as "real" happiness. Diana was you. Diana was me.

The old woman died and made the news by contrast. There were mourners and there were flowers, but few could or would take the death of a Mother Teresa to heart. No one likes to identify with the old, the poor, the diseased and the dying.

We prefer Diana's approach: Use wealth, power and position to raise money for the cause of the unfortunate. Put on a benefit concert, write a song, do a media event, wear a ribbon. See them for a brief moment while the cameras roll, and share in their pain for a special second. Give them a taste of our royal acceptance—a special, shining sacrament before they die. This is our modern version of sainthood.

But to give this up and do something like actually *live with them* without reward or return is a strong indication of some kind of insanity.

No, there will not be many hot aftermarket books on Mother Teresa.

A HUNGER FOR REALITY:
THE NO-BULL GENERATION

For the congregation of hypocrites shall be desolate, and fire shall consume the tabernacles of bribery (Job 15:34, *KJV*).

For parents raised to be polite at the expense of reality, this generation of kids is often rude. Never expect a softened version of the truth from a GenNexter. They are candid, frank, blunt, straightforward, honest, tactless. You want to know what one of them thinks? Don't ask unless you really want to know—in the raw. All too often they will tell you exactly what they see, even if you don't like it. Revival, too, brings reality back to a world of social convention and truth modification. The word for "actor" in the Bible is the word "hypocrite."

Item from the TV show "Politically Incorrect": Bill Maher is interviewing his usual polarized mix of guests, including a comedian known for his biting invective and cynicism. Bill speaks of a church in Pensacola where he reports, "They say a wind blew there and the Spirit came, and now thousands of people line up each day to see what God is doing."

Bill comments to the comedian: "That's more than come to your shows, George."

Cynical Comedian: "All religion is toxic, and Christianity is particularly toxic."

Token Right-Wing Conservative: "It's a good thing you're criticizing Christians and not Jews or Muslims for their religion, or you'd be dead."

Maher, closing the segment later, says, "Well, I think we need this. We've got adulterous bomber pilots and a flashing President. I rest my case."

This no-bull generation was raised from babyhood on the best advertising, most researched hype and most expensively produced fantasy ever, giving them almost by default an inner sensitivity to what is real, good and lasting. If "hypocrite" is another word for "actor" in the Bible, can you hope to fool a generation that grew up watching the best actors in the world?

Larry Tomczak tells of a young evangelist who got on a bus after a long week of a local crusade, paid his money to the bus driver and went to sit down. He realized as he counted his change that the driver had not charged him enough and, embarrassing as it was, went back up to the driver to tell him. "You didn't charge me enough," he said. "You gave me too much change."

"I know," said the bus driver. "I was in your crusade last night. I just wanted to see if you really lived what you say you believe."

JUDGEMENT IN THE HOUSE OF GOD: TRUTH WILL OUT

The time has come for judgement to begin in the house of God. The Church was rightfully shocked at the exposure of some of its highest-profile Christian leaders on television, and the enemies of the Lord had a heyday over it. I was in Australia then, being interviewed during a series of youth meetings that were the largest the little town had ever seen.

After the standard questions about money and crowds, the interviewer, hoping to capitalize on the current controversy, named one of the fallen TV evangelists and fired his last question: "What do you think about—?"

There was less than five seconds of interview time left. There was no time for a comment on the dealings of God with His backslidden Church, of justice and grace, repentance and forgiveness, on what is wrong and what is right in a world that no longer believes in absolutes.

I said, "It's about time you guys in the media said immorality was wrong. You never said it before."

Cut. Finish. Move quickly on to another item. But this story still goes on. God always deals with His Church first. "You only have I known," He speaks by the prophet to His backsliding nation (see Amos 3:2). "Therefore I will judge you." We know so much more than the world; it is right that we be held up as hypocrites and sinners if we pretend and if we sin. *Knowledge equals responsibility.* We are supposed to be examples to the world, and when we hold back, the world falls apart.

To him who knows to do good and does it not, to him it is sin. But when the world gets through pointing its finger with glee to sin in the Church, publishing it abroad for all to see and condemn, the world may awaken to the fact that three other fingers point back to itself. In condemning others for wrong, it may in fact reiterate what is right, and by judging God's people it will also judge itself and its own heroes. The judgement you judge shall also judge you. Your own words will be a witness against you. In such ways kings are convicted by the critics of their own culture.

> Oh Lord, please light the fire
> That once burned bright and clear.
> Ignite the lamp of my first love
> That burned with holy fear.

— Keith Green, "Oh Lord, You're Beautiful"

BELIEVERS: POSTMODERN SNOW WHITE AND THE PSYCHIC HOTLINE

Got a brand-new story though you've
heard it a time or two
'Bout a Prince who kissed a girl right out of the blue.
Hey that story ain't no tale to me now,
For the Prince of Peace has given me life somehow,
You know what I mean.

— Second Chapter of Acts
"The Prince Song"

Annie Herring of the group Second Chapter of Acts has often talked about how, as a child, she would sing Snow White's make-a-wish love song from the early Disney animated film *Snow White and the Seven Dwarfs*. "Some day my prince will come, one day I'll find my love," young Annie would sing, just wishing someone would come to take her away from the sadness and colorlessness of her life and whisk her into her own fairy-tale romance. That Prince indeed came, just as He has come to many lonely and friendless orphans over the centuries.

It is interesting to note that in Walt Disney's version of the story, the once-beautiful queen becomes a witch through pride and hatred, that Snow White is spared from death because of her virtue, and that in the final showdown between the evil queen and the brave defenders, it is a judgement from heaven that fells the evil one—and that in the place she falls *you never hear her hit bottom*. We should also observe that when the kiss of the prince resurrects Snow White, he carries her on his white horse to his castle, not on the earth but *in the sky*.

But that was long ago as fairy tales go, and Disney films have changed a lot since those times. Now our animated heroes are the likes of Aladdin, a jobless Islamic thief who whispers a lewd comment as he climbs to meet his chosen princess in her bedroom; Pocahontas who, unlike the real-life twelve-year-old who became the first Christian convert among the Native Americans, converts explorer John Smith to animism and follows the spirits of the forest; Simba the Lion King, who finds courage in an astrological revelation from his dead father; and Mulan, who saves an Oriental prince through the advice of her ancestral spirits.

So, what of it? Snow White is dead. Now we can make up our own fairy stories. Even better, everybody's story is true!

As G. K. Chesterton pointed out, when we give up believing in God, we become not atheists but magicians. We don't believe in nothing; we believe instead in anything and everything. We not only believe in God and the devil, in heaven and hell, but also in angels, demons, agents Scully and Mulder, Atlantis and Area 51. We are the postmodern society, and *everything* is okay.

NOT EVERYTHING IS GOD

The voice of the Lord divides the flames of fire (Psalm 29:7).

"What shall be the sign of Your coming," asked the disciples, "and of the end of the world?" Earthquakes, Jesus mentioned. Wars and rumors of wars. Famines. Terrible persecution. Then He said, rather cryptically, "When you see the fig tree putting forth its leaves, know that summer is near" (see Matthew 24:32).

Arthur Custance has pointed out that in the metaphor of Scripture while the *vine* represents the political history of a nation and the *olive* represents its real spiritual history, the *fig* always represents the religious history of that nation.

The sign of the fig tree is actually evidence of massive religious interest at the dawn of the end of the age. This postmodern generation is not in danger of irreligious denial but *religious deception*. As Francis Schaeffer warned us, the *name* Jesus has become the enemy of the Person of Jesus. There is nothing more devastating to faith than the enemy who comes in the clothing of a friend. Only a visitation from the Real can expose the sophistication of the false. The Bible warns of spiritual wickedness in high places.

> Take careful heed to yourselves, for you saw no form when the Lord spoke to you at Horeb out of the midst of the fire, lest you act corruptly and make for yourselves a carved image in the form of any figure (Deuteronomy 4:15,16).

During the days of the hippie movement in San Francisco, I met a girl in Golden Gate Park who was there reading a Bible. She had the Word open to the book of Revelation, and she was smoking a joint. This in itself was not too strange a sight in those times. Sometimes hippies would drop acid or blow weed and get off on the apocalyptic imagery. (Ever wonder why there aren't more movies made from Revelation? Even Spielberg would find the book a challenge!)

"I see you're reading a Bible," I said to the girl in the park. "Do you enjoy reading the Bible?"

"Oh, yes," she smiled at me. "Praise God, I'm a Christian."

"I noticed you were reading the book of Revelation. Have you read much of Revelation?"

"Yes," she said. "It's my favorite book."

"Did you ever read the parts that speak about the dangers of witchcraft and sorceries? I wonder if you've ever seen the root meaning of the word translated "sorceries" there. Did you know that it is the word *pharmakia*, and it has as one of its key meanings to induce religious experiences through the use of drugs?"

"Oh, yes. Somebody already explained that to me."

"Then you know that the use of drugs as any kind of aid to worship is wrong in Scripture."

"Yes."

"So you know that using drugs is a sin."

"Oh, yes."

"Then could you explain something to me? Why are you still toking on that joint?"

"Oh, you don't understand," she said. "My body is sinning, but my spirit is worshiping God."

I wondered which one of her was talking to me.

When the Lord Is Not in the Fire

And after the earthquake a fire, but the Lord was not in the fire; and after the fire a still small voice (1 Kings 19:12).

Yea, the light of the wicked shall be put out, and the spark of his fire shall not shine (Job 18:5, *KJV*).

Not everyone who lights a candle to God belongs to Him or has authority to handle His work. In a day of religious deception, some false worship may prove both final and fatal. Inheritance here does not matter; you can be the child of the high priest and still fall under the fire of the judgement of God. Nadab and Abihu, the sons of Aaron, offered up to the Lord fire other than that which was commanded by God. "So fire went out from the Lord and devoured them, and they died before the Lord" (Leviticus 10:2).

What is the chief evidence of religious deception? An independent spirit—someone who lights his own fire.

Satan was a church kid. He sat under the ministry of the greatest Pastor, Prophet and Priest of all. His Leader was beyond reproach, wholly and utterly pure without wrinkle or blemish, utterly blameless in anything and never stumped for an answer. No one could ever accuse God of delivering a sermon that lacked content or of being insincere or irrelevant or simply unable to communicate His message well. Satan came from a perfect congregation without a single hypocrite, where no one had ever given a single bad example or blown it in any way at all. Even the choir at his church was out of this world—they all sang like angels!

Yes, the devil was once a church kid, but he still went down. And how did he fall? Satan did not get into trouble by annexing the heavenly collection and running off with an angelic-looking secretary to Alpha Centauri. His problem was *an independent spirit.*

Stay a learner. Never covet for yourself a place or position God didn't call you to. God opens the door to the servant-hearted learners, those who esteem others better than themselves and are not afraid to bury their dreams for another's. Honor one another in word and deed, says the Lord, that there be no division in the Body (see 1 Corinthians 12:23-25). "Those who honor Me I will honor" (1 Samuel 2:30).

Some years ago I had to give counsel to a friend who had been offended by another well-known and respected spiritual leader. In previous years, when my friend's ministry was small and relatively unknown, the leader of this other major ministry had encouraged them, supported them and spoken well of them. Now, with their work grown greatly and much better known, this older leader had begun to criticize, withdraw from them and unaccountably reject my friend's ministry.

My friend was devastated and uncertain how to respond. "Rebuke not an elder, but entreat him as a father," Scripture said, and did not seem to give as a condition the fact that his criticism seemed unfounded and unfair (1 Timothy 5:1, *KJV*). What had happened between them that led to this state of affairs? In searching Scripture for a possible approach, I was struck afresh by two little phrases in the passage of 1 Corinthians 12 that deals with unity in the Body. "The eye cannot say to the hand, 'I have no need of you,'" Paul says there (v. 21). He also speaks of honoring each part of the body, however significant or unseen, that there be no division in the Body (vv. 23-25).

Three things became clear:

1. If a man attempts to pull out his own eye, he is insane; he has become somehow disconnected to his head;
2. Disunity is caused by dishonor; and
3. The way to dishonor is to express in attitude or in words, "I have no need of you."

When the smaller ministry needed the encouragement of the larger, they conveyed their appreciation of his help. When they became bigger, their failure to acknowledge a debt of love and honor to their former benefactor created a division that drove and directed his initial criticism and eventual cutting off. Dishonor creates division. *Honor.* Honor one another.

> Look, all you who kindle a fire, who encircle yourselves with sparks: Walk in the light of your fire and in the sparks you have kindled—*This you shall have from My hand: You shall lie down in torment* (Isaiah 50:11).

Sometimes we can't see what God is doing all around us. We cry out for light, yet see nothing but darkness. We hear no voice and see no flame. The darkness of God is a key curriculum in the school of the Spirit. Neither sin nor ignorance nor demonic attack, it is the temporary withdrawal of the sense of God's presence—an action designed to wean us away from the expectation of reward for every good action. Many of us go through such darkness; it is an essential part of our training. But there comes in the darkness a strong temptation to take up our own torch when we receive no immediate answer. God can speak in darkness, and in the absence of light the pupil opens up to a never-before-known level of sensitivity so that previously ignored light suddenly becomes dazzling.

Just do what He said before you entered into the darkness: Lean on His love and don't light your own fire.

ALL IN THE FIRE:
DEVOTION MEANS TO THE DEATH

The sinners in Zion are afraid; fearfulness has seized the hypocrites: "Who among us shall dwell with the devouring fire? Who among us shall dwell with everlasting burnings?" He who walks righteously and speaks uprightly, he who despises the gain of oppressions, who gestures with his hands, refusing bribes, who stops his ears from hearing of bloodshed, and shuts his eyes from seeing evil: he will dwell on high; his place of defense will be the fortress of rocks; bread will be given him, his water will be sure (Isaiah 33:14-16).

When hymn writers of the past penned lyrics like

> When I survey the wondrous cross
> On which the Prince of Glory died,
>   My richest gain I count
> But loss and pour contempt on all my pride;
> Forbid it Lord that I should boast
> Save in the death of Christ my God,
>   All the vain things that charm me most
> I sacrifice them to His blood

and

> Would He devote that sacred Head for such a worm as I

they understood something we have largely lost today with our five-minute chicken-soup "devotionals" and our round-the-table morning "devotions" of a Bible reading and prayer.

They knew that devotion meant *to deliver something to the death.* Jesus calls us first not to a feast but to an execution, not to an exciting event but to a funeral. And the execution and funeral are our own.

THE WORD UNDER FIRE:
THE BOOK THAT WOULDN'T BURN

"Is not My word like a fire?" says the Lord, "and like a hammer that breaks the rock in pieces?" (Jeremiah 23:29).

Throughout its history, people have tried to burn the Bible. But fire has a way of surviving fire. In our day, especially in the West—where we have more than thirty translations of Scripture, so we can disobey God in Greek, Hebrew and Aramaic—physical burning is largely useless. We prefer to burn the Bible with a black-colored bead in a Jesus Seminar vote or a casual, condescending remark about its words being "true for you but not for me."

Yet amid all the hype and marketing, the hunger is there in the new breed. It is one of the most neglected areas of youth ministry today. Kids want to study and discuss *the Bible*. They are sick of groovy games and cutesy attempts by adults to accommodate the revelation of God and of shtick-polished presentations in culturally correct, chamfered time slots for the sake of convenience. Kids are tired of the Church's fascination with the trimmings. They want to know *what the Book actually says*.

David Hoyt was a friend of mine during the Jesus Movement. He met the Lord in the strangest way—in the basement of the Rhada Krishna Temple in San Francisco. In the spirit of universal religion, David had allowed a street preacher to conduct a Bible study for his Krishna group while the Swami was back in New York.

Now David was no newbie; he had studied intensely Babaji, Lahyira Mahasiah, Sri Yukteswar and Paramahansa Yogananda. He knew the teachings of the Maharishi with his golden promise of Cosmic Consciousness in just five years. He had studied the mystical teachings of "The Fourth Way" with Gurjieff and Ouspenksy, Zen Buddhism under Dr. Suzuki and Katiguri, and Sri Rama Krishna with Swami Vivikanda.

David's path had required not only book learning but also many hours of daily meditation and chanting. He wanted earnestly to find a new life. And then this street preacher walks in and teaches there is only one Mediator between God and man—Christ Jesus (see 1 Timothy 2:15). If what the preacher said were true, David had been deceived for three and a half years!

I'll let David tell the rest of the story for himself:

I finally cornered the preacher in the Krishna kitchen and asked him what right he had to say this and be so narrow-minded. He spoke: "You have been possessed by a demon of divination. But God is faithful and within three weeks you will be taken out and you will know the true and living God." *Wow!* In an instant I knew there was a battle going on, and I felt an actual force and spirit inside me that caused me to tell him to leave and never come back.

After being in the Temple for a while, I saw there was always dissension. I could never put my finger on what I felt was really wrong, but it was there. It just began to dawn on me that I was doing the very thing I hated about being a Catholic altar boy: going through all these rituals and never really knowing what was going on. In the Krishna temple I would take food and place it before these three wooden idols and worship Krishna, offering this food to him.

Then the words of the boy who had begun to tell me about the Bible came back to me and how he said to stop chanting for just one day and ask Jesus if He wasn't the true Savior and Christ. He told me how Jesus warned about the vain repetitious prayer the heathen make, and the many false prophets and teachers that would come and try to deceive the people in the last days (see Matthew 6:7,8; 24:23-27). All these things came back and plagued my thoughts.

One night as I was lying on my bed in the basement of the Krishna temple, I saw a vision. This was really strange for me, but it was like I was taken into another realm to see something fantastic. As I looked, I found myself looking over a huge marketplace where people were buying things and talking. Every different race and people that had ever lived on earth were represented, and I could hear the many different languages being spoken in the background.

All of a sudden there was a great noise and all the people stopped moving. There was complete silence. The blast of the noise was so loud that everyone cringed at the power of it. As this happened, I saw different people in this large multitude begin to raise their hands upward, and as they did they began to sing together in one beautiful language. When I heard this I knew they were singing to God, and their hands went higher and higher until they were actually lifted off the ground physically.

Then I looked up and as big as the sky I saw the ARMS and FACE of Jesus taking all of His children home. Wow! It was at this moment I got the largest shock of my life, for I saw that my feet were on the ground along with many others who had been deceived. I had always believed that Jesus was the greatest Guru or Avatar of the Ages, but now I realized He must have been more. I can honestly say that this was the first time in my life when I actually began to pray. I didn't have words or my own ideas, but I inwardly pleaded and asked God to please show me the Truth at any cost.

I began to dislike the rituals that I'd been practicing. I just wanted to escape that chanting that had possessed me.

It was seven A.M., on the morning Kirtan was in full swing in the Krishna Temple, when smoke began billowing out of the basement where I stayed. I ran down the steps with other Krishna people close behind. I felt a supernatural power come over me as I viewed this large Universal Altar with every religion represented burning to the ground. Stepping close to the altar, I grabbed the only remaining book that hadn't already caught on fire. It was the Bible. No one had to tell me what was happening as I opened it to a page that revealed that Jesus Christ, the true Light of the world, was setting me free (see John 3:16-21).

I felt clean and whole for the first time in my life, and I realized that Jesus had suffered and died in my place that I might live and know the true God. The true and living God, Jesus Christ of Nazareth. I was able to rip off my prayer beads and know the evil spirit that was trying to make me act so holy was gone forever, and that the blood of Jesus was now my righteousness and His resurrection from the death was my victory.

Only one way? How narrow-minded!

DREAMERS: FROM PLAYSTATIONS TO PROPHECY

"And it shall come to pass in the last days, says God,
that I will pour out of My Spirit on all flesh; your sons
and your daughters shall prophesy, your young men
shall see visions, your old men shall dream dreams."

Acts 2:17

The language of the Holy Spirit is
dreams and visions.

— Dr. David Yonggi Cho,
pastor of the largest church in the world

The Lord has showed me I have to go places
no one has ever been before to see things
no one has ever seen before.

— Abi, a young friend from the United Arab Emirates
with a missionary evangelist call of God on his life

You are the most visual generation ever to emerge in Western civilization. You've grown up in a time when visual technology has truly come into its own. You learned from Mario the plumber and Sonic the hedgehog how to survive and win in a cyberkinetic world, and to this day the quickest way to get something through to you is to show you a picture.

BEFORE VIDEOS THERE WERE VISIONS

> Then I looked, and behold, a whirlwind was coming out of the north, a great cloud with raging fire engulfing itself; and brightness was all around it and radiating out of its midst like the color of amber, out of the midst of the fire (Ezekiel 1:4).

You are not the first generation in history to see things visually, but you *are* the first to be able to see a repeatable, controllable vision on command at your leisure. Unlike Ezekiel, whom God lifted up in the Spirit by the forelock of his head and held hanging over a valley of extremely dead people (see Ezekiel 37), you do have a choice of what movie you'll be watching this weekend on video, DVD, cable or pay-per-view. Unlike young Isaiah, you don't have to wait until a king dies to see something amazing (see Isaiah 6:1).

The prophetic gift is the ability to see the future in the present and in the past. Kings of the mightiest nations of all time were spoken to in this fashion that has since been technologically imitated in machines and software now available at any video retailer. Nebuchadnezzar, Pharaoh and Belshazzar all had dreams and visions, and men of God spoke to tell them about what they saw and what it meant according to the Almighty Himself.

Paul said, "I am ready" (Acts 21:13). There are two main Greek words that mean to be ready for something. One suggests the readiness that comes from physical or mental preparation, like a fighter on the eve of a world title bout or a tennis or golf pro awaiting the last round of an tournament. That word for ready means: "I have done my homework, I have put in the time, I have honed my reflexes. Whatever comes my way will receive an unflinching, automatic answer." But that is not the word Paul used for "ready" here.

He used another word, *prothumos*, meaning "to have a future mind." Paul was talking about *future thinking*. He was talking about living in what was coming. He saw what was going to happen and was already preparing himself for the day he would face it.

One of the strangest parables told by Jesus is the parable of the five wise and the five foolish virgins. In it, both groups had lamps that were lit. Both groups were invited to the wedding feast and were waiting for the bridegroom. The story says that when one group of watchers realized their oil had begun to run out, they went to get some more. The sad part of the story is that while they were gone, the cry went out that the bridegroom was coming, and all those that had waited so long went into the feast to meet him. The five girls who had gone came back to find a shut door and a shocking exclusion from the party.

There are many odd things about this story, not the least of which is that at no wedding I've ever been to did the bridegroom wait so long to show up for his own wedding party. Who could blame the girls for having to go and get more oil when he seemed to take so long? It hardly seems fair that they were shut out. Apart from their having to make an emergency stop, there was no difference between those finally locked out on the street and the other five in the room.

There is in fact only one difference, but it is critical. The five that made it in not only had their lamps and their oil and their virginity, but they also had a *future mind*. They asked the unspoken questions: *What if he takes longer than anyone thinks? What if he, for his own reasons, delays his coming? What must we do to get ready for such a possibility? What can we do while we wait for him?*

The only difference between the ones who made it in and those who did not is preparation for a delayed future promise. The future belongs to those who plan for it. GenXers must get over their curse of hopelessness and take hope in God. *Those who do not plan for the future will not own it.*

FEAR OF THE LORD AND THE FIERY PRESENCE

"Sensational" and "phenomenal" are words used to describe the early Pentecostals. "Sensational" because, understandably enough, they really "sensed" God's presence when He visited. They shook, they moaned, they trembled, they worshiped and spent inordinate amounts of time on the floor. Faith for them was something they *felt*, not just an intellectual belief in the truth revealed in the Bible. "Phenomenal" because they knew when God visits man, things really begin to happen. The tongues of men and angels, once unknown to them, spread the astonishing word to the city, the nation and the world: Christ has come for His own.

> And they will tell it to the inhabitants of this land. They have heard that You, Lord, are among these people; that You, Lord, are seen face to face and Your cloud stands above them, and You go before them in a pillar of cloud by day and in a pillar of fire by night (Numbers 14:14).

> And the sight of the glory of the Lord was like devouring fire on the top of the mount in the eyes of the children of Israel (Exodus 24:17, *KJV*).

> Then there appeared to them divided tongues, as of fire, and one sat upon each of them (Acts 2:3).

What is the *first thing* God commanded the children of Israel to do? Some might say obey Him. Many would say love Him. Others might say serve Him. And, of course, these are all things Israel was called to do. We cannot go wrong by obeying, loving and serving God. But none of these is the *first* thing. And today that first thing is the most neglected thing.

We speak about God's laws, His love, His service, and we urge people to give themselves wholly to these as evidence of being true followers of the Lord. But without the first thing, all these true things lose their power to move our hearts. The first thing God commanded Israel was to *fear Him* (see Deuteronomy 6:1-20).

All the revelations of heaven are rooted in holy terror. There is no difference in the Hebrew words between that slavish fear we are commanded to conquer and the awful Presence that made the worlds with a word. Yet He may come at any time and reveal His true nature to people who have played the fool too often to take Him seriously. Fear Him, says the Scripture.

Rick Howard, a pastor in California, speaks of his early years when he received his first vision of Jesus. A ministry friend had been studying the judgement seat of Christ, and he urged Rick to read the book of Revelation where it speaks of Jesus as the One who judges the worlds. Rick reluctantly did so, and fell asleep reading it. *And then he had a most vivid dream.*

He tells how as a boy his parents always called him "Rick" or "Ricky," unless he was in trouble. Then he would be called "Richard." Although called to preach, like some of his friends he had drifted somewhat from his original zeal for God, though he had not left the ministry like another friend who had abandoned it for money and gone on to manage a used-car lot.

In his dream, he suddenly found himself on a great plain. Beside him on one side was his friend. At his other side was a dear old woman, a saint that he knew well. Neither said anything. All around him, as far as the eye could see, were people—people by the thousands, people standing in silence, all looking in one direction. Rick turned to see what it was they were all staring at as one.

Coming toward him, swiftly, silently and holding a great flaming torch high in his hand was a white-robed Figure, hair brighter than light. But it was not the hair or the clothes that struck terror into Rick's heart. It was the Figure's *eyes*. His eyes did not look like eyes at all, but like twin lamps of burning fire.

The Figure came on in total silence, swept His eyes past Rick and his friend and stopped in front of the old woman. In front of her was a small pile of what looked like grass. The Figure called out her name, and the torch in His hand came down upon her pile. There was a *whoosh!* and a flash, and all that was left in front of her was a pile of glittering coins and gems. She lovingly held them out to Him, but He was already turning to Rick's friend standing there beside him with a much bigger pile in front of him. Those eyes swept right past Rick and burned into the face of his former friend. The Figure called his friend's name. The same burning torch swept down, there was another *whoosh!* and smoke, but this time all that was left was a black ring of burnt ashes.

His friend let out one single cry, a cry that chilled Rick's blood, a cry that seemed to echo across the plain to be heard by every living soul: AAAAAAHHHHH!!!!

Then, to his terror, the Figure turned to face Rick. All he remembers now is the sight of those terrible eyes, eyes that saw through him, and dimly the sound of the burning torch as it flashed down toward his own small pile in front of him. And then the Figure said, "Richard . . . ."

Rick fell out of bed covered in sweat and then consecrated himself to the ministry that he has since never surrendered to compromise or conceded to failure. "Knowing, therefore, the terror of the Lord," says the Scripture, "we persuade men" (2 Corinthians 5:11).

THE ONE FIRE NEVER FORBIDDEN

My heart was hot within me; while I was musing, the fire burned. Then I spoke with my tongue (Psalm 39:3).

Then I said, "I will not make mention of Him, nor speak anymore in His name." But His word was in my heart like a burning fire shut up in my bones; I was weary of holding it back, and I could not (Jeremiah 20:9).

There is one fire God will never forbid you—the fire of His presence in your innermost being to tell a cold and dying world that His truth and His mercy are still available and that Jesus is alive.

A young man named Billy has preached in all kinds of embarrassing places: on crowded planes just after landing, with the aisles jammed by people waiting to get out; movie theaters just before the main feature starts; upon a lunch table in a cafeteria; under the flag by the entrance as kids left school; from the back of his station wagon in the parking lot. He is not alone. More than two and a half million teenagers now gather round the flagpole before school on at least one day each year to publicly tell the world, "I belong to Christ."

Who shall the Lord call? "Who among us shall dwell with the devouring fire?" (Isaiah 33:14). He recruits from the ranks of those who come from families who no longer care. He calls the peculiar teenagers, the outcasts who fuel the talk shows that push the boundaries of media schlock. Solitary, unsmiling and stubbornly un-silent, they are held up to public ridicule and rejection as sad spectacles by the Springers and Sterns of our time. Shock jocks and outlandish interviewers draw on a pool of people who hurt so much and are literally damned angry. They're "mad as hell," and they don't care who knows it.

Not so some parents, always smiling and saying the polite thing regardless of its truth or consequences. This blunt new breed think and feel too much. Such strange ones are considered dangerous.

> When Jesus came to Golgotha, they nailed Him to a tree.
> They drove great spikes through His hands and feet
> And made a Calvary.
> Red were His wounds and deep,
> For those were crude and cruel days
> And human life was cheap.
>
> When Jesus came to our town, we simply passed Him by.
> We never hurt a hair of Him, we only let Him die.
> For men had grown more tender;
> They would not cause Him pain.
> They only just passed down the street
> And left Him in the rain.
>
> Still Jesus cried, "Forgive them
> For they know not what they do,"
> And still it rained the winter rain
> That drenched Him through and through.
> The crowds went home and left the streets
> With not a soul to see,
> And Jesus crouched against the wall,
> And cried for Calvary.
>
> (G. Studdart-Kennedy poem that Billy read to students
> in his high school cafeteria at lunch)

"Revival," said one British evangelist, "is not going down the street with a big drum, but going back to Calvary with a great sob." Those forgiven much, love much.

I heard the voice of the Lord, saying: "Whom shall I send
. . . who will go for Us?" (Isaiah 6:8).

THE FOURTH MAN IN THE FIRE

And the angel of the Lord appeared unto him in a flame
of fire out of the midst of a bush: and he looked, and,
behold, the bush burned with fire, and the bush was not
consumed (Exodus 3:2, *KJV*).

Fire does not always mean destruction. To the one who is cold,
fire is warmth. To the lonely, fire is comfort. To the powerless,
fire is strength and energy. To the one walking in darkness, fire is
light.

The children of Israel understood. Though they were afraid
in the wilderness, they knew that as long as the cloud went before
them during the day and the fire was there in the night, they were
guarded and sheltered and kept from other horrors that might
come to a people without a home or country—because they had
the promise of the One who lived in the fire.

Then the Lord will create above every dwelling place of
Mount Zion, and above her assemblies, a cloud and
smoke by day and the shining of a flaming fire by night.
For over all the glory there will be a covering (Isaiah 4:5).

When you pass through the waters, I will be with you;
and through the rivers, they shall not overflow you.
When you walk through the fire, you shall not be burned,
nor shall the flame scorch you (Isaiah 43:2).

Nebuchadnezzar threw the three young men in the furnace. Cream of the chosen, these Hebrew boys had passed Babylon's own global leadership training program with the highest scores ever recorded, a quantum leap above all others Nebuchadnezzar had culled from his captives around the world. He did not fully know then that their success was due to an unflinching commitment to the God of their fathers and that they had simply rewritten his training material to conform to the laws of the true God. All he knew on that day was that three boys had ruined his display of universal homage to the great gold idol made in his image, that when the music played over the crowds assembled to give him worship they would not bow.

> Then Nebuchadnezzar, in rage and fury, gave the command to bring Shadrach, Meshach, and Abed-Nego. So they brought these men before the king.
>
> Nebuchadnezzar spoke, saying to them, "Is it true, Shadrach, Meshach, and Abed-Nego, that you do not serve my gods or worship the gold image which I have set up? Now if you are ready at the time you hear the sound of the horn, flute, harp, lyre, and psaltery, in symphony with all kinds of music, and you fall down and worship the image which I have made, good! But if you do not worship, you shall be cast immediately into the midst of a burning fiery furnace. And who is the god who will deliver you from my hands?" (Daniel 3:13-15).

They stood before the licking furnace fired with bitumen and forced air, so hot it killed even soldiers conscripted to push into it transgressors stupid enough to defy the commandment of the king of the known world. But the three young men did not offer much in the way of a defense. "We have no need to answer you in this matter," they said. "Our God whom we serve is able to deliver us from the burning fiery furnace, and He will deliver us from your hand, O king. We do not serve your gods, nor will we worship the gold idol you have made" (see vv. 16-18).

Then Nebuchadnezzar was full of fury, and the expression on his face changed toward Shadrach, Meshach, and Abed-Nego. He spoke and commanded that they heat the furnace seven times more than it was usually heated. And he commanded certain mighty men of valor who were in his army to bind Shadrach, Meshach, and Abed-Nego, and cast them into the burning fiery furnace (Daniel 3:19,20).

But Nebuchadnezzar was in for a surprise. The warriors who got near enough to throw our heroes into the furnace were themselves consumed by the fire. So the furnace was certainly hot enough to destroy three stubborn, willful, foolish young men. But when the king looked into the furnace to see that his will had been carried out, he shouted, "Look! . . . I see four men loose, walking in the midst of the fire; and they are not hurt, and the form of the fourth is like the Son of God" (Daniel 3:25).

When the music plays and the whole world falls down to worship, every now and then some will stick out of the crowd by refusing to bow. Such people are ready to die, and yet sometimes when they will not bow, God sees to it they will not burn. From such choices without compromise even kings who rule the world receive a witness.

Then Nebuchadnezzar went near the mouth of the burning fiery furnace and spoke, saying, "Shadrach, Meshach, and Abed-Nego, servants of the Most High God, come out, and come here." Then Shadrach, Meshach, and Abed-Nego came from the midst of the fire. . . . The hair of their head was not singed nor were their garments affected, and the smell of fire was not on them.

Nebuchadnezzar spoke, saying, "Blessed be the God
of Shadrach, Meshach, and Abed-Nego, who sent His
Angel and delivered His servants who trusted in Him,
and they have frustrated the king's word, and yielded
their bodies, that they should not serve nor worship any
god except their own God!

"Therefore I make a decree that any people, nation, or
language which speaks anything amiss against the God
of Shadrach, Meshach, and Abed-Nego shall be cut in
pieces, and their houses shall be made an ash heap;
because there is no other God who can deliver like this."

Then the king promoted Shadrach, Meshach, and
Abed-Nego in the province of Babylon (Daniel 3:26-30).

For four boys the overturning of their world had begun with the
invasion of their country by the armies of the most powerful king
in all of recorded history. Year after dangerous year, the backslidden nation of Judah had turned a deaf ear to the warnings of
God. His judgement finally fell. In 605 B.C., Nebuchadnezzar,
undisputed ruler of the ancient world, conquered Judah. He
crushed the nation and orphaned its young people, cutting them
off from their homes and families and putting an entire generation of teenagers under the power of an alien culture. Everything
they ever knew and loved was swept away.

Devotion to the true God all but vanished as the young of
Judah were introduced to a civilization filled with the most
astonishing array of beauty, technology and spiritual options the
world had ever seen. Few past commitments survived. Babylon
usurped the hearts, minds, lives and worship of an entire generation.

Nebuchadnezzar assimilated the cream of every nation he
conquered into the Babylonian civil service. He chose the very
best of Judah's youth to contribute their gifts and talents to the
empire of Babylon. Once selected, they entered into a program of

intensive reeducation in the language, literature and lifestyle of the ruling world power. Nothing was permitted to distract them from their studies. Their names were changed to include the names of pagan deities. Their identities and destinies were swallowed up and reassigned by Babylon. They were even to forget they were Jews, that they were ever God's servants.

Yet astonishingly, a small number stood up for God. Almost alone in the days of the Babylonian exile, this covenantal remnant was represented by four teenagers, moral wonders of the ancient world: Daniel, Hananiah, Mishael and Azariah.

Daniel was about 14 years old when he was taken from his home and forcibly marched to a strange land. He was subjected to strong indoctrination and surrounded by powerful and jealous enemies who plotted against his life. Yet he not only survived three different governments, but was also considered so significant and irreplaceable that he continued to serve in each one in exactly the same position of power and responsibility. The hardships Daniel and his three friends had to face demonstrate the real truth about godliness: True spirituality never depends on things being easy.

What happened to these young men has happened again in your time. The pressures they faced and the program they were put on are here again. You face the same choices presented to Daniel and his three friends. The spirit of Babylon is alive, dangerous and dominant once more in the ruling civilizations of our century.

Daniel's decision to obey God in all things could result in only one practical outcome: He reached the utter highest and best he was capable of achieving. "In all matters of wisdom and understanding" Daniel was found to be *"ten times better"* than any in the realm (Daniel 1:20). If they had no grace or courage to refuse idolatry, Daniel would never have had the power to stand firm in the lions' den, nor would his three friends have survived the fiery furnace.

Daniel's band put God first. They dared believe His ways were
not only excellent but also *extraordinary*. They took the king's
own goals and turned them into an adventure in showing the
world the glory of their God. He in turn honored them and
stirred up in their lives gifts, privileges and authority they never
dreamed they could have.

You stand now where they stood. Dare to do what Daniel did
and you will never be the same again. The God who made them
great for His glory is with you now, unchanged and unchanging,
ready to show the world once more, through you, what it really
means to live. He awaits only another Daniel band. What He did
then He can do again.[1]

A few young men dared stand up for God and truth in their
time. Because they didn't bow, the Fourth Man who joined them
in the fire saw to it that they didn't burn.

NOTE
1. From the introduction to *The Daniel Files*, the free, electronically distributed
   life-skills manual for GenX, available along with other training materials
   from our website at http://www.moh.org.

COCOONERS:
PAIN SHELTERS AND
HOLY CYBERJACKS

Pain abounds in our world. There is so much hurt today that kids take shelter wherever they can find it. Sometimes they're lucky enough to find refuge in a friend. Many must look instead to drink or drugs. Some years ago a presidential wife launched a well-meaning campaign to reduce drug use among children and teens in America. It was called "Just Say No." Unfortunately it was largely powerless. A promotional campaign couldn't seriously diminish the drug problem because at heart the drug problem is neither about peer pressure nor advertising. It's about pain.

It is, of course, painfully true that kids today face enormous pressure to be users of some sort. This generation takes its drugs and drinking *seriously*. U.S. Centers for Disease Control and Prevention record more than 100,000 alcohol-related deaths each year. In 1994, 16.3 percent of kids between the ages of 12 and 17 were actively using alcohol. Liquor companies spent more than one billion dollars in 1995 to advertise beer, wine and liquor, two-thirds of that on television commercials. And 7.3 percent of teenagers use marijuana on a regular basis; nearly as many as smoke regular cigarettes (*U.S. News & World Report*, July 7, 1997, p. 57).

Kids are drinking and drugging daily and don't give a rip about statistics like these or the many well-intentioned warnings.

Facts in a postmodern world mean almost nothing. Postmodern thinking says, *What is true is only what is true for me. Just because someone else got hurt or killed doesn't mean the same thing will happen to me or anyone else I know.*

Proverbs 31:6 says, "Give strong drink to him who is perishing." Even in Old Testament days, when people were dying, when they hurt so badly they couldn't stand it anymore, they were given some kind of painkiller. Did you know there was a biblical justification for the use of drugs and drink? Does that shock you? Not only that, you are probably quite a drug user yourself.

When did you last visit your dentist? Did you have a cavity? Was it—perish the thought—a front tooth? The dentist all but strapped you into his chair, put a "sucker" in your mouth and told you to let him know if it hurt, all the while knowing that if you did say anything it would sound like "uurg-ga-hrmmm." He pulled back your lip and took a hypodermic with a long needle in his hand and . . . .

Unless you are a Buddhist practicing some form of "trans-in-dental medication," I know you didn't just say "No."

Most U. S. babies today are born under the influence of drugs. They grow up using drugs as advertised on TV to ease pain, suffering and mild congestion. Almost no one now is truly living drug-free. The purpose of a narcotic is to take away pain, to numb the hurt. How many of you just said "No!" to that dentist's needle? Did you say: "What's in that needle? Is that a drug? It is? Well then, no. I saw a Nancy Reagan commercial, and I will not take your drugs. No. No. No."

Or did you say, "Yes! Hit me again, Doc, I can still see you"?

We will never deal with the drug problem until we find some reliable, fundamental way to take away the pain that people live with every day. You cannot easily say "No" until the hurt stops. And there *is* Someone who can do just that, Someone who will not give you platitudes and powerless advice when you are dying on the inside and must find a way to stop the hurt before it kills you.

THE ULTIMATE PAINKILLER

He is despised and rejected by men, a Man of sorrows and acquainted with grief. And we hid, as it were, our faces from Him; He was despised, and we did not esteem Him. Surely He has borne our griefs and carried our sorrows; yet we esteemed Him stricken, smitten by God, and afflicted.

But He was wounded for our transgressions, He was bruised for our iniquities; the chastisement for our peace was upon Him, and by His stripes we are healed (Isaiah 53:3-5).

If ever someone could justify using drugs to ease His pain, it was Jesus, who died in a more terrible way than we can ever imagine: hurting without and within, taking on His holy heart the sins of the entire world.

Crucifixion is the most awful form of execution ever devised by mankind. Criminals convicted of capital crimes against the Roman government were stripped naked and paraded before the world, suffering the shame and humiliation of helpless exposure to those who had come to jeer or weep as the condemned carried his own cross to the place of execution. The hands and feet of the criminal were nailed to the cross and the cross erected for all to see. Often the victim's bones were dislocated by the shock of the cross dropping into its mounting hole, the spikes further ripping their flesh. The crucified man slowly strangled to death, the weight of his own body crushing the life out of him. Without food or drink, his very life draining away, the dying man would push himself up on the cross with his last ounce of strength just to take a breath before finally giving in to the inevitable. If he hung on too long, a soldier would come along and break his legs to end his struggles.

It sometimes took a strong man three days to die, and Jesus was a strong man, a carpenter by trade. Yet the centurion did not have to break His legs to finish Him. Pilate marveled that He was already dead (see John 19:32-38; Mark 15:44). It was not the cross that killed our Lord Jesus. It was not the pain or the thirst or suffocation that took His life. He said that no man could take His life from Him, that He would lay it down instead. *So what was it Jesus died from?*

In one awful instant, the spotless Lamb of God took onto His heart the sins of the whole world. He who had never sinned from the time He first opened His baby eyes felt the shock of all the hurt, the guilt, the shame and defilement of billions with no other chance of pardon before a Holy God. He became sin for us, who knew no sin (see 2 Corinthians 5:21). When the Roman centurion believed Jesus was dead, he thrust a spear into His side, and there came out blood and water—a sign of agony so intense it literally ruptured the cardiac muscle. *Jesus died of a broken heart.*

And Jesus knew what it would be like before they nailed Him up there. There, dying for us, in all His hurt and suffering, He was offered a potent drug mixture to dull the pain. And He refused it.[1] He was "in all points tempted as we are, yet without sin" (Hebrews 4:15). The one time anyone might have been justified in using drugs or drink, He turned it down. He did it for your sake.

GOD'S INCREDIBLE HULK: STRENGTH FROM ANOTHER WORLD

And the Angel of the Lord appeared to the woman and said to her, "Indeed now, you are barren and have borne no children, but you shall conceive and bear a son. Now therefore, please be careful not to drink wine or similar drink, and not to eat anything unclean. For behold, you shall conceive and bear a son. And no razor shall come upon his head, for the child shall be a Nazirite to God from the womb; and he shall begin to deliver Israel out of the hand of the Philistines."

And He did a wondrous thing while Manoah and his wife looked on—it happened as the flame went up toward heaven from the altar—the Angel of the Lord ascended in the flame of the altar! When Manoah and his wife saw this, they fell on their faces to the ground.

So the woman bore a son and called his name Samson; and the child grew, and the Lord blessed him (Judges 13:3-5,19,20,24).

God's sunshine, the boy born by a miracle and destined from birth to save his nation, was given three great covenants to keep. He was to never cut his hair; he was to never touch the dead; and he was to never touch wine.

For all we know, Samson may have been skinny like me. Delilah never said, "Sam, what gym do you work out in? You've got great lats and pects." She said instead, "What is the secret of your great strength?" The long hair no doubt seemed weird to some; they may have whistled at him and called him a girl—for a few seconds, at least until they saw the power from another world fall upon him.

The prohibition against dead bodies we understand. Why should the guy who is the life of the party, the cool riddler at the feast and the hot young hope of the nation hang out with the dead? But the kibosh on wine was the kicker. *He was to put no chemical into his mouth or body that might inflame his mind or boost his body artificially or chemically.* God wanted no one to think his great strength came from anywhere but heaven.

Other than dealing with terminal pain, why do people still drink today? People who drink look for a lot of things in the bottom of a glass: to be happier, braver, perhaps to feel they are smarter. (Drunk people have opinions on everything; they certainly talk more and louder as the evening wears on.) When you get drunk you not only begin to lose your balance; with it also go your inhibitions, your reservations and your fear.

When the Day of Pentecost had fully come, they were all with one accord in one place. And suddenly there came a sound from heaven, as of a rushing mighty wind, and it filled the whole house where they were sitting. Then there appeared to them divided tongues, as of fire, and one sat upon each of them. And they were all filled with the Holy Spirit and began to speak with other tongues, as the Spirit gave them utterance.

And there were dwelling in Jerusalem Jews, devout men, from every nation under heaven. And when this sound occurred, the multitude came together, and were confused, because everyone heard them speak in his own language. So they were all amazed and perplexed, saying to one another, "Whatever could this mean?" Others mocking said, "They are full of new wine."

But Peter, standing up with the eleven, raised his voice and said to them, "Men of Judea and all who dwell in Jerusalem, let this be known to you, and heed my words. For these are not drunk, as you suppose, since it is only the third hour of the day.

"But this is what was spoken by the prophet Joel: 'And it shall come to pass in the last days, says God, that I will pour out of My Spirit on all flesh; your sons and your daughters shall prophesy, your young men shall see visions, your old men shall dream dreams. And on My menservants and on My maidservants I will pour out

My Spirit in those days; and they shall prophesy'" (Acts 2:1-6,12-18).

On the Day of Pentecost, the little crowd that had been huddled in the upper room at the command of Christ knew what they were waiting for. Before them was a commission of human impossibility: Go to all the world, preach and reach it for God. Jesus had said He would not leave them alone, but now He was gone. They needed something to keep them brave in the face of terrible opposition, to give them wisdom greater than any they had ever known, to keep them full of joy when the world was dark and frightening, to take away their timidity and doubt. They wanted Jesus back with them.

It had been a scary ride, walking with the Son of God into situations where only crazy men go. They never knew the meaning of prayer and trust until He put them in places they couldn't handle and sent them on missions they couldn't carry out and bade them do things no one could actually do. Now He was gone, but He said they were to wait for Another, the One who would be to them what He was when He walked beside them and showed them how to act and live.

And then as promised, He suddenly came. The crowd that spilled out of the upper room around nine o'clock that morning looked for all the world like they had just been to the party of the year. People seeing them and hearing them reached the same conclusion: These guys were stoned out of their minds! They were loud, all talking at once, acting unbalanced and uninhibited. And they were so full of joy that it had to be new wine.

Peter did not contradict them. He stood up to tell them they were not drunk *the way others thought they were drunk*. The same Bible passage that forbids us to be drunk with wine commands us to be filled with the Holy Spirit (see Ephesians 5:18). This is intended not as a contrast but as a comparison. In a world like ours, who doesn't need some way to stay happy, smart, brave and even a little unbalanced every day? Who doesn't need a stiff drink at a place where everybody knows your name?

Yours is a generation *desensitized to feeling anything*. Raised in a climate of both real and fantasy horror, assaulted on all sides by violence, death and terror, kids have learned to construct emotional cocoons around their hearts and minds, to drug it out or translate what they see and feel as a game, a movie, a special effect. If you have to face it alone and without help, the terror will kill you. This is why kids at a horror movie will sometimes laugh or cheer while their parents are hiding behind their hands. And it doesn't stop with the movies.

Like the German camp commandant in *Schindler's List*, kids today will kill, not to save their lives or to intimidate a victim or an enemy, but for fun—out of sheer *boredom*. These are not zombies, creatures without the ability to reason, but what we might call "Frombies"—people without feeling, cut off from the emotional feedback that tells them the truth about pain in the world.

Drugs and drink help keep their cocoons intact. Rage and hurt make it thick and tight. Many of these kids have never been held or touched or hugged in their whole lives. The closest thing to love they have ever known is raw sex, and the closest things to real feeling they experience are the aphrodisiac of anger and the wine of rage.

How do you touch a generation like this? With words, when they are sick of words? With explanation, with analysis, with rational presentation, with cold, correct and comprehensive argument? Do you want to try it on a street kid who would shoot to death his own best friend?

Hey, fool, do you want to die?

NOT DRUNK, BUT FILLED

And Hannah answered and said, "No, my lord, I am a

woman of a sorrowful spirit: I have drunk neither wine nor strong drink, but have poured out my soul before the Lord" (1 Samuel 1:15, *KJV*).

When Hannah went into the Temple to ask God for a miracle child, she prayed in such distress of heart that she acted stoned and crazy. Eli the priest thought she was drunk and rebuked her. Sometimes prayer that touches God seems to spiritually unperceptive eyes as a violation of all that is religiously right and proper. Someone with true devotion in the sanctuary of God can be misread as dull-witted or even demonic. Eli didn't see the sin in his own sons as they slept with women who came to the Temple and violated the holy place with their lust and greed. But he rebuked Hannah, just a simple lady who loved God. Hannah got her son from God—Samuel—and he became one of Jehovah's great prophets and heard His voice clearly when Eli the religious leader did not.

An embarrassing characteristic of today's awakening is the direct bypassing of critical analysis to allow the Holy Spirit to move at will. This is the manifestation in revivals today that inspires in some religious critics "manifestations" of their own. Self-appointed authorities on revival and cultish behavior, when faced with admittedly strange phenomena, can themselves behave in most ungracious ways, attacking and slandering the nature and character of the work in question and those involved in it. They make scholarly and detailed reference to the dangers of mindless behavior and duly quote scriptures on doing things "decently and in order" (1 Corinthians 14:40). And they broadcast dark warnings of the dangers of deception when we turn over our services and Christian meetings to something so patently beyond our own control.

And almost without exception, *they miss the point.*

God does what He does without our permission. When He moves, it is always in line with His Word and what He has said and done in history before. This we know from His changeless nature and character. But those who smugly speak against what He is doing in our time with this particular generation are in danger of writing off the Hannahs and the Samuels, the fractal edges of God's calling today. God does not have to check in with us to see if we approve first before He does what He wants to do. Revival by its very nature is not under the control of the Church; the Church is to come under the control of God. And the man who thinks His move is always explicable has never really been in it.

A SPLIT PULPIT IN HOUSTON

Tommy Tenney is a friend, the godly son of a well-respected church leader who understands the work of the Holy Spirit and has spent a lifetime seeing God move among people. Tommy was a guest speaker at Christian Tabernacle, a multithousand-member Houston church where Pastor Richard Heard and many of the elders had been praying for revival for some years. On this particular morning, the worship and praise in the early service intensified to a level they had seldom felt or seen before. Tommy said it was like the bridal train in Princess Diana's wedding: It came, and then it kept on coming and coming.

The pastor turned to Tommy and asked if he was ready to speak. "To tell you the truth," he replied, "I'm half afraid to go up there. I think something is going to happen." The pastor said he felt he should read from Scripture and that he had a word from the Lord. Going up to their new high-tech, space-age, unbreakable acrylic pulpit, Pastor Heard opened his Bible to 2 Chronicles 7:14 and read aloud. "The word of the Lord to us is to stop seeking His benefits and seek Him. We are not to seek His hands any longer, but seek His face."

Then something happened that has since sent shockwaves through the Church. Though there was no rain or lightning outside, there came a clap like thunder, and the pulpit Pastor Heard was standing in front of split in half. He was thrown back, knocked out on the floor, unable to move for hours. The pulpit was thrown forward, landing in two pieces in the carpeted altar area, forever unusable. The presence of God was so strong in the church that people arriving in the parking lot outside for the second service fell out of their cars as they opened the doors to get out. The meeting went on and on into the evening and the next day and continued week after week as people met God, were saved, delivered, healed and restored.[2] It made an impression on Tommy he will never forget. When I asked him a year later what it was like, his eyes filled with tears. "I can scarcely speak about it," he said.

One of the last walls of separation in the Church is the artificial division that exists between the "clergy" and the "laity," the idea that ministry is for the religious professional and the audience comes simply to be religiously entertained for an hour. The pulpit is a modern equivalent of the veil of the Temple, that thick curtain that separated the presence of God from His people in Old Testament times, the veil that was rent at the death of Christ forever.

Looking at the ruins of their "unbreakable" pulpit later, the church in Houston came to a conclusion about the shocking visitation that had changed their lives: God does not mind being emcee at our services, but He really wants to be in charge of the whole thing.

Item: In the wired society of the New Millennium, futurists predict that the ultimate stimulus will be neither drink nor drugs, but a *cyberjack*—direct electrical stimulation of the neural pleasure centers of the brain. The same futurists postulate that the device delivering a cyberjack will need to be equipped with a timer. Monkeys wired in this way will continue pushing the button that pulses their pleasure centers until they die of starvation or thirst—even with food laying all around them. There is nothing more powerful than a direct stimulus of the brain that bypasses all critical and analytical functions to directly touch the mind and feelings.

The strange happenings in Houston are not unlike those being reported in revivals breaking out around the world. So what's going on? I believe we are witnessing something we tend to rebel against in Western society, where our order of learning is the direct opposite of the biblical model. In Scripture, God speaks (revelation), we do it (practical service and obedience) and *then* He explains it—maybe (illumination). But in our intellectually idolatrous culture, we *first* demand an adequate explanation. Then if we understand it and approve, we think about doing it. And we hope finally to become "spiritual."

Charles Finney, summarizing at the end of his life an astonishing ministry of revival and evangelism, said that the one thing he would do most differently if he had to start all over again would be to hold out the *truth* of God and call people to *obedience* first, and only explain later for the benefit and edification of God's dear children. Finney noted this was the Bible's example—trust God and His Word at face value and get used to doing things simply because God said them, without always wanting to know why He said them. Reverse the process, he said, and you will raise a generation that is "cynical, fault-finding, nit-picking, rationalistic and critical, that either hold very lightly to divine things that do not admit of ready theological or philosophical explanation or reject it entirely."

Welcome to the Western world at the edge of the twenty-first century.

DISCERNING THE TRUE MOVE OF GOD

Who is wise and understanding among you? Let him show by good conduct that his works are done in the meekness of wisdom. But if you have bitter envy and self-seeking in your hearts, do not boast and lie against the truth. This wisdom does not descend from above, but is earthly, sensual, demonic. For where envy and self-seeking exist, confusion and every evil thing are there.

But the wisdom that is from above is first pure, then peaceable, gentle, willing to yield, full of mercy and good fruits, without partiality and without hypocrisy (James 3:13-17).

The *Bible's test of truth* looks for an honest attitude, a spirit of humility, servant-heartedness and learning. How can you know in a postmodern world who is really right with God? First, does the person in question have a *servant heart* for Jesus? Is there a spirit of humility and the true mark of a disciple, a learner's attitude? What is the *fruit* of his or her life? Does it bear the character of Christ?

Does what this person says match what God has already said? There is another wisdom that poses as truth but in actuality comes from the pit of hell. It is marked by bitterness, strife, rancor, fights and every evil work. If this spirit and work of the flesh marks a so-called religious authority, it *utterly disqualifies* him or her from valid comment on spiritual deception, because that person is, according to the Bible, already deceived.

And the Jews marveled, saying, "How does this Man know letters, having never studied?"

Jesus answered them and said, "My doctrine is not

Mine, but His who sent Me. If anyone wants to do His
will, he shall know concerning the doctrine, whether it is
from God or whether I speak on My own authority. He
who speaks from himself seeks his own glory; but He who
seeks the glory of the One who sent Him is true, and no
unrighteousness is in Him" (John 7:15-18).

Jesus told us how we can know the truth in teaching. None of
us personally owns the truth, as if we are the ultimate and final
authority on it; we first must do what God says and the knowing
will follow. Thus it has always been in the Bible: *Correct perception
follows practical, loving obedience.* Many critics who claim to be
authorities on God and His Book, when put to this elementary
test in their own lives, would utterly fail.

A. W. Tozer, that godly, prophetic evangelical pastor who
steeped his life in Scripture, devotional church history and thousands of hours of prayer, warned of the dangers of bibliolatry. He
said when we Christians sing, "Beyond the sacred page, I seek
Thee Lord," we are not saying we no longer need the Bible, but
that memorized and quoted verses alone will never change our
lives. *Disobeyed truth deceives.*[3]

Jesus said to the Pharisees of His day, who arguably knew the
Torah better than any other religious leaders of their time, "You
search the Scriptures, for in them you think you have eternal life;
and these are they which testify of Me. But you are not willing to
come to Me that you may have life" (John 5:39,40). It is very possible to love our knowledge of the Bible without loving God. A
man full of religious argument can also be full of religious
demons.

If what is going on is indeed a genuine but strange work of
God, I believe we are witnessing something from heaven designed
for a generation otherwise impervious to argument and rational
discussion, something both loving and terrifying and powerful
that cuts through all cynical layers of self-defense and screened

rejection, something divinely calculated to touch a generation numbed to everything and anything *except a Christian cyberjack from the Holy Spirit.*

Kids who once argued and fought and hated everything done to reach them are being touched directly and powerfully. I have seen bored church kids cynically immune to every kind of appeal and altar call utterly laid bare by a bolt from heaven that broke them suddenly and sent them weeping to their knees. I have seen street kids who have fought and shot and lived in utter hardness busted by an encounter with the Holy Spirit that in one single touch took away all their hurts and defenses and opened their hearts to the gospel of Christ.

I know there are exceptions and deceptions and that some things are not of God, just the reaction of people who have never experienced the true presence of God. There's not always an appropriate way to behave in a visitation. Scripture says, "Where no oxen are, the crib is clean" (Proverbs 14:4, *KJV*). If you want a nice, antiseptic, sanitized situation, *don't put anything alive in it.* Live cows make a mess.

Revivals are messy, dangerous, and have slippery floors. There has never been a revival in history that had no problems, no criticisms and no opposition. Why should this one be an exception? I can offer no other explanation or argument for what I have seen except that by its fruit and long-term effects it has led bitter, untouchable kids to bow their knees to the power of Christ and transformed them into new creatures. I can only say that our sovereign God, who knows the hearts and minds of this generation better than the world ever will, is doing something wonderful when all the Church's own efforts and explanations have failed.

Like the man born blind in Scripture, these kids are coming to Jesus when they don't even know who He is, having their eyes opened first and then seeing Him as God in a *divine regeneration without explanation.* Like the man born blind, this generation has no theological explanation for its healing, but is absolutely and joyfully ready to testify to miracles to established religious critics and cynics even before it fully sees its Savior (see John 9:1-38).

Like the man born blind, the arguments their healings will engender may cause splits in the Church and fights among religious leaders, and may even get them kicked out of church for telling the truth of what happened to them.

But they will be joined by Jesus, and He understands.

NOTES

1. Two drinks were sometimes offered victims of crucifixion: vinegar to quench thirst (see Matthew 27:48; Mark 15:36; John 19:29,30) and a potent alcoholic, narcotic mix of gall and myrrh, which was refused by Christ (see Matthew 27:34; Mark 15:23).

2. Tommy Tenney, *The God Chasers*, (Shippensburg, Pennsylvania: Destiny Image, 1998), pp. 5-11.

3. See James 1:22-26. In a culture where we can easily obtain much religious information without required biblical character and attitude, the possibility of self-deception is overwhelming. Those who seem to be religious but show an aggressive, fight-picking, independent spirit by an uncontrolled, arrogant tongue deceive their own hearts. Scripture says this man's religion is useless. See also Galatians 6:6-10; James 2:9-13; 3:1-13; 4:6-12. We are known by our fruit.

EDGERS: GATTACA, BRAVEHEART AND EXTREME EVERYTHING

> "Every man dies.
> Not every man really lives."
>
> —From the movie *Braveheart*

> Looking unto Jesus, the author and finisher of our
> faith, who for the joy that was set before Him
> endured the cross, despising the shame, and has sat
> down at the right hand of the throne of God. For
> consider Him who endured such hostility from
> sinners against Himself, lest you become weary
> and discouraged in your souls.
> You have not yet resisted to bloodshed,
> striving against sin.
>
> Hebrews 12:2-4

They wear the label proudly: *extreme*. It touches everything in life, from the clothes they wear and the things they do to their faces and bodies to the sports they play and the images they model. To a Baby Boomer generation raised on concepts like *balance* and *moderation* and *caution*, such behavior is highly unacceptable. To put it plainly, their lifestyle is far too extreme.

But the world has never been moved by the mild or the moderate. Balance can be bad. Mad people rule the world, and the choice we are presented with in the closing days of history may not be between the mad and the sane, but between holy or unholy madness. They said of the apostle Paul that "much learning" had made him mad (Acts 26:24). Of Jesus, the living God in flesh, they said He was "out of His mind" (Mark 3:21). That kind of madness moved the arrogance of world rulers, marked the key epochs of history and wrote the book of Acts. If we would move the world today, we must choose between holy and unholy madness. Hence, God is recruiting from the ranks of the rejected.

"You Are Not Radical Enough!"

At a recent Mario Murillo crusade, there was a young punker sitting in the front row dressed to impress in ozone-warrior gear, fully spiked and ringed under his green anti-gravity-gelled hair, daring the evangelist to make a comment on his appearance. Mario looked him over and then looked him in the eye and said, "You are not radical enough!"

> Quenched the violence of fire, escaped the edge of the sword, out of weakness were made strong, waxed valiant in fight, turned to flight the armies of the aliens (Hebrews 11:34, *KJV*).

> So Elijah answered and said to the captain of fifty, "If I am a man of God, then let fire come down from heaven and consume you and your fifty men." And fire came down from heaven and consumed him and his fifty (2 Kings 1:10).

Radical is not multicolored hair. Radical is not cool clothes and designer shoes. Radical is not a shaved or ratted head, a tough tattoo or a pierced lip. Radical is not a skateboard grind, a rollerblade move or a killer wave.

Radical is knowing how to—and being willing to—get to the root of it all. It's the ability to cut to the core of what is right or wrong with the world. Tom Skinner said, "Yesterday's radical is today's conservative because he's so busy conserving the things he got by being radical, he can't afford to be radical anymore."

A radical life is knowing God so well you can pray once and the heavens close for three years and then pray again and see fire fall from the same sky, yet still be a man of passions like any one of us (see 1 Kings 17,18). Posers are plenty.

We are badly in need of some real radicals.

The Man with the Fire and the Fan

"I indeed baptize you with water unto repentance, but He who is coming after me is mightier than I, whose sandals I am not worthy to carry. He will baptize you with the Holy Spirit and fire. His winnowing fan is in His hand, and He will thoroughly clean out His threshing floor, and gather His wheat into the barn; but He will burn up the chaff with unquenchable fire" (Matthew 3:11,12).

Fire or a fan. Get hot or get cold. He's not interested in anything in between. Just as all computer code breaks down to a 0 or a 1, it's either one or the other. We haven't yet learned that obedience in Scripture is digital. (Only learning is analog.) With God, doing what He says is either yes or no, never something in between. The guts and the glory of the gospel are tied directly to this kind of expected surrender. When Jesus speaks to people, He talks to them as if He *expects* them to leave everything and follow Him.

Poor Mrs. Zacchaeus. She looks out the window one day to see Jesus and the twelve disciples walking up the path toward her house, with her husband running just a few steps ahead. "Guess who's coming to lunch!" he says excitedly. She's excited too, but for a totally different reason.

As he comes into the kitchen, she gives him that look that every husband knows and hisses at him, "*Zach!* Are you crazy?! What do you mean inviting Jesus and the disciples for lunch without even bothering to tell me?" Then she shifts gears. "Oh, come in, Jesus! It's so nice to see you." Then to Zach under her breath, "Why didn't you tell me He was coming?"

"I didn't invite Him," says Zacchaeus. "He just invited Himself" (see Luke 19:5).

Who is this Jesus? He walks up to people who are just minding their own business and, without so much as an introduction, He calls them out of it forever. His sermon is not even a "three-pointer"—just two words. The invitation has no music, no altar call, no bulletin. Just two words: "Follow Me." And how does He carry out the delicate task of follow-up and care for the new convert? Take a guess. "Follow Me."

Who is this Jesus? He talks as if He owns the whole universe! He speaks as if what you do with what He says will be the most important thing you ever do in life. Who *is* this Jesus? *He talks like He's God or something.*

You want extreme?

He told the rich young ruler to sell all he had and give it to the poor, that he would have treasure in heaven and to follow Him. The rich young ruler didn't and dropped out of history (see Luke 18:18-23).

He told the woman at the well that if she drank the water He offered her she would never thirst again. She did, went back to her village and brought half of those who knew her back to Him (see John 4:1-42).

He told a deeply religious man, Nicodemus, that unless he was born again he would never see the kingdom of God. Nick braved the censure of his peers and discovered a new life (see John 3:1-8; 7:50).

He told those who followed Him that unless they ate His flesh and drank His blood they could have no part in Him. It is not recorded whether or not they thought He meant it only metaphorically or whether they thought He had actually called them to be cannibals, but it *is* recorded that from that time, many went back and walked with Him no more (see John 6:48-66).

He told Peter, His disciple, exactly how He was going to die and then said, "Follow Me." Listen to His words: "If anyone desires to come after Me, let him deny himself, and take up his cross daily, and follow Me" (Luke 9:23).

He said there are only two roads, one that leads to heaven and the other that leads to hell, and that only a few would take the straight and narrow road, while many would head for the broad way (see Matthew 7:13).

He said that you could tell a tree by its fruit and that no normal tree puts out a mixture of good and bad fruit, no matter what theologians or psychiatrists may say (see Luke 6:43,44).

He told stories about sheep and lost sons to sinners who loved Him (see Luke 15) and asked religious leaders unanswerable questions that made them angry (see Matthew 12:12-14).

He said a poor lady's last coin was worth more than a whole wad a rich man dropped into the collection plate (see Luke 21:1-4), and that a weeping hooker would be remembered for wasting her life's savings to pour perfume over His feet (see Mark 14:3-9).

He broke up every funeral He ever attended by raising the corpse from the dead. He raised a dead boy, a little girl, then a man who had been dead three whole days (see Luke 7:12-15; 8:41-56; John 11:11-44). Then He did it all over again at His *own* funeral, even though the Romans had posted a guard and the religious leaders had sealed the grave with a boulder.

You want extreme?

No one in history ever was born like Jesus, lived like Jesus, talked like Jesus and loved like Jesus. Not even His enemies could find fault with Him. He defies comparison, because there is nobody else you can put in His class. Period. He split history in half. He not only claimed to be God, but *showed* His kingdom every way you can ask to anyone who really wanted to see it. When you come to Jesus, He doesn't give you options or alternatives, just a core decision: "Follow Me."

If you do, you are a disciple.

If you don't, you drop off the map forever.

And that, my friend, is extreme.

RADICAL SOLUTIONS TO RADICAL BATTLES: DEALING WITH SIN IN A DECAYING CULTURE

> "If your hand or foot causes you to sin, cut it off and cast it from you. It is better for you to enter into life lame or maimed, rather than having two hands or two feet, to be cast into the everlasting fire. And if your eye causes you to sin, pluck it out and cast it from you. It is better for you to enter into life with one eye, rather than having two eyes, to be cast into hell fire" (Matthew 18:8,9).

Plucking out a straying eye or cutting off a wandering hand is certainly more radical than most people would ever choose, unless they were miscreants in a Muslim court who held very strictly to the old penalties for adulterers and thieves. Most of us would prefer a fine or, even better, a sharp warning not to do it again. After all, if this were carried out to the letter, we would live in a seriously large society of blind people and multiple amputees.

If you have a choice between losing an eye, a hand or a foot, which would you choose? Few of us want to even think about making that sort of choice. Anyway you cut it, it's just too painful and permanent to consider. Jesus said what He said so that you and I would understand just how serious sin is and just how terrible our future will be if we do not take His words seriously.

There are other ways to cut yourself off from evil, though none of them as scary as cutting off your hand or gouging out your eye. Seen in the light of permanent death to our most significant body parts, what does it matter if we say good-bye to a cherished friend, habit or commitment that gets in the way of our devotion to God?

In the great days of evangelism, missions and revival two hundred years ago, the Church would call for repentance from five things:

1. *Sin*, a self-centered attitude of heart and life;
2. *The Flesh*, an addictive focus on emotional gratification through our five senses;
3. *The World*, that beautiful, orderly cosmos around us without God at its center that demands our time and loyalty;
4. *The Devil*, any demonic, occultic involvement; and
5. *Our Own Righteousness*, the "good" things of our lives we have never surrendered to God.

Back then this was considered utterly essential and foundational to Christian living. Now in many churches in the West, you should consider yourself fortunate if you're called to repentance *at all*. No wonder our converts rarely change the world. They may never experience "a repentance not to be repented of."[1]

> [They] have cast their gods into the fire; for they were not gods, but the work of men's hands—wood and stone.

Therefore they destroyed them (2 Kings 19:18).

Ernie was hooked on porn. For years he fought a losing battle, even after becoming a Christian. One day he learned that true
repentance means to really see, hate and forsake our sin.
Returning to the store from which he usually bought his magazines, he purchased again the latest copy of the glossy garbage
that had long fed his addiction. After paying for it, he held the
magazine out to the owner over the counter and asked, "Is this
my magazine?"

"Yes," came the hesitant reply.

"If it's mine, can I do what I want with it?"

"Yes."

"Good." And with that, Ernie tore the magazine to shreds
and dropped it all over the counter. "It's stuff like this that helps
kids like me go to hell," he said and walked out, never to return.

God's laws are descriptions of reality. They are not just good
ideas. The Ten Commandments are not called "The Ten
Suggestions." Real trust in God involves giving up anything and
everything that vies for our allegiance to Christ. The true
"edger"—he who lives on the edge—has set his heart on surrender
to Jesus and will cut off without pity anything that would hurt
His heart.

How radical does the radical life have to be? Remember the
eye, the foot and the hand.

"He who finds his life will lose it, and he who loses his life
for My sake will find it" (Matthew 10:39).

I got a call from a girl one morning at around 5:30. She told
me she was thinking of killing herself. (Strange, I was thinking
the same thing.) She told me after some minutes of aimless conversation how much of her life she had messed up and that she
wanted to die. I told her she was probably right, that her life was

indeed a terrible mess, that she probably hadn't even told me half of what was wrong with her, and that she really did deserve to die. I told her I understood her wanting to kill herself. However, if she was just going to use a razor blade or a gun or suck a car's tailpipe she wouldn't really be able to get it right.

I said to her, "All you will do is kill your body, and you'll just be stuck with the shame and the guilt and the pain forever. What you need is an executioner, someone who can do the job properly." I told her I could help her. I told her I knew somebody that would not only finish her off for good, but do it so she never had to live with the hurt and guilt again. I told her if she was really ready to die, I could introduce her to Him. And then I talked about Jesus and His call to deny ourselves, take up our cross and follow Him. I told her that when someone becomes a Christian, that person becomes brand-new inside, and he or she is not the same anymore, but a new life has begun. I finally prayed with her and let her go into God's hands.

Two weeks later, I got a great letter from the ex-corpse. She wrote, "When I told my friends I called you and you told me I not only deserved to die, but I needed to die, and that you would help me do it, they couldn't believe it. But you were right. I met the Executioner, and I'll never have to live my old life again."

"For to me to live is Christ, and to die is gain" (Philippians 1:21).

THERE IS NO GENE FOR THE HUMAN SPIRIT

Gattaca is the film story of two brothers set in the not-too-distant future, a time when the genetic code of the human genome has been cracked, and everyone can be advance-typed or identified by a tiny sample of their skin, hair or a drop of blood. Jobs are assigned by predicted health and intelligence quotients, and no one may aspire to a position beyond his or her physical capacity.

The older of the two brothers, Vincent, was conceived naturally and is by genetic type a disaster. He has poor vision and a
terminal heart defect, fit (according to his code) only for a jani-
torial position. His perfect brother, Anton, genetically presorted
to be almost anything he wants, is a criminal investigator. At
tremendous personal risk and cost, Vincent pulls off an imagina-
tive, highly illegal pretense to get into the occupation of his
dreams—going into space with the Gattaca Aerospace
Corporation. On the very eve of Vincent's launch, Anton discov-
ers his brother's charade.

Threatened with exposure, Vincent challenges the superior
Anton to another endurance swimming race, like the first one he
ever won against his brother when he summoned the strength to
beat the smug Anton so thoroughly that he had to save Mr.
Perfect from Mr. Deep. Both plunge again into the ocean, swimming toward the open sea, going as far as they can before one or
the other gives up and has to return to shore.

And again, heart problems and all, Vincent, the one society
deems the weaker of the two, wins. Back on the shore, having
once again rescued his perfect kinsman from drowning, Vincent,
who will go into space the following day against all odds, lets his
brother in on his secret.

"Do you want to know how I did it?" he asks. "Do you want
to know how I beat you? This is how I won: I never saved anything
for the return."

NOTE

1. Bill Gothard calls them "non-optional principles," that we be people under
   divine life purpose, responsibility, authority, suffering, self-acceptance, forgiveness, moral purity, yielding our rights to God's ownership. A non-
   optional principle is simply another name for a life lived under mercy in
   commitment to the commands or laws of God.

LEPERS: MARILYN MANSON MISSIONARIES

Maybe I should become a Christian, like all the
Christians say who are praying for me.

— Marilyn Manson,
in a 1998 *Rolling Stone* rock videography.

And the leper in whom the plague is, his clothes shall
be rent, and his head bare, and he shall put a covering
upon his upper lip, and shall cry, Unclean, unclean.
All the days wherein the plague shall be in him he
shall be defiled; he is unclean: he shall dwell alone;
without the camp shall his habitation be.

Leviticus 13:45,46, *KJV*

In Bible times leprosy was considered such a terrifying affliction
that it was often not thought of as an ordinary disease at all, but
a special judgement of God. Lepers had no property, no position,
no power, no inheritance, no influence, no insurance. When a
leper lost his face and his fingers, with it went his family, his

fortune, his friends and his future. Within a few yards from a leper, all pity died.

If anyone embodied a parent's nightmare in the 1990s, it was the lead singer of the rock group Marilyn Manson. Satanic, sensual, sacrilegious and downright scary-looking, Manson's name is the intentional fusion of America's famous: Marilyn Monroe, the gorgeous sex-goddess of the '60s who died in strange and suspicious circumstances, and Charles Manson, the '70s California cult leader whose frightening "family" murdered, among others in a Hollywood home, the pregnant wife of the director of *Rosemary's Baby* and later tried to assassinate a president.

"I am the devil," said Charlie Manson in his own defense at his trial, as he looked into the camera with his mad eyes. Everyone believed it. Everybody saw what he and his minions had done to those they had murdered. "I am Jesus," he said and shocked the nation even more. But the real shocker was his last word: "I am America."

Why is that so shocking in a culture that believes there are no real rights and wrongs, that all there is is the truth of what ought to be, that there is nothing more important or significant than anything else? What exactly did Charlie Manson mean, if not that he only summed up in himself, *I am all America is and I really live what America believes*?

Nearly thirty years later, Marilyn Manson terrifies middle America, his act embodying everything heartland America despises. Yet tens of thousands of kids have been drawn to his concerts like moths to a flame and his following is numbered in the hundreds of thousands. Birds of a feather flock together, the old adage says. There is something in what Marilyn Manson is that strikes a chord with GenX.

Watching him one day in a TV interview, even without his morbid makeup, I was struck by how much Manson looked like a dead man.

A Leper Has Nothing to Lose

In times of war, disease and famine, even people not needing to be pronounced clean by priestly proclamation had difficulty staying alive. For a leper, whose very existence depended wholly on the mercy and charity of others, a time of disaster was a virtual sentence of death.

Four lepers trapped at the gates of besieged Samaria were the worst of losers, wholly the wrong people trapped in the wrong place at the wrong time. Supernaturally enough, they became heroes (see 2 Kings 7:3-11). Times change, but God does not. History recycles and the future waits for those who will go to the enemy camp with nothing to lose. Cities still die from a lack of lepers.

> Therefore thus says the Lord God of hosts: "Because you speak this word, behold, I will make My words in your mouth fire, and this people wood, and it shall devour them" (Jeremiah 5:14).

Do you know what makes a modern terrorist so terrifying? They are already dead men. They are not afraid to die, because they have already been to their own funerals. You cannot frighten terrorists with death when they already have played it out a thousand times. Former Soviet leader Nikita Kruschev once addressed a parade of young graduating Communist soldiers, men whom he might someday call on to pay the price to see their ideology triumph in the world. His speech was simple, short and unforgettable. He said, "You are all dead men. Now go into the world and prove it."

THE BEST THINGS COST THE MOST: THOSE WHO WIN THE FINAL WAR

So Abraham took the wood of the burnt offering and laid it on Isaac his son; and he took the fire in his hand, and a knife, and the two of them went together. But Isaac spoke to Abraham his father and said, "My father!"

And he said, "Here I am, my son."

Then he said, "Look, the fire and the wood, but where is the lamb for a burnt offering?" (Genesis 22:6,7).

He who did not spare His own Son, but delivered Him up for us all, how shall He not with Him also freely give us all things? (Romans 8:32).

It's hard to give up something that hurts you, especially when you've lived with it so long it seems like a familiar friend. It is harder still to give up something others would call "good" when God has put His finger on it as an idol in your life that must go. But it is hardest of all to give up something God Himself gave you, when that gift has meant so much more than anything else in your life. How do you surrender up the life of your son? How can God ask for the darling of your heart? How can He possibly understand how much it would cost you to do this thing He asks of you?

They had flown over the Aucas many times, dropping food and gifts to this violent people no one had ever been able to reach with the gospel. Finally it seemed as though the Aucas looked forward to their visits, waving as they flew over the clearing. Now the three young missionaries were going to make their first attempt to meet the Aucas face-to-face. They had a brief service with their wives and children before they set out through the jungle. They sang the old hymn:

We rest on Thee, our shield and our Defender;
We go not forth alone against the foe,
Strong in Thy strength; safe in thy keeping tender
We rest on Thee and in thy Name we go.

They prayed again and set out on foot, carrying food and gifts to the Aucas. Their wives and children waited for hours. The morning wore on to a long afternoon; then evening brought twilight to the jungle. They waited, but the young missionaries never came back.

Finally, near nightfall, the pilot of a plane sent to the meeting place confirmed the worst. He spotted the bodies in and near the river clearing where they had always seen the Aucas. All three had been killed. Speared to death, they apparently never had a chance to say anything.

The American government reacted predictably, ordering evacuation for the safety of its citizens. The grieving widows and children were returned home to pick up the pieces of their shattered lives. "What a waste," some said. "It's not right that we let people go to such savage areas of the world. For their own good, missionary activity in such areas should be prohibited."

Betty Eliot was visiting at the home of one of her friends, Wendell (Wendy) Collins, a director of Teen Teams for Youth For Christ. Trying to comfort her, Wendy asked how she was coping with the death of her husband.

"Wendy," said Betty, "Jim didn't die in the jungle."

"I know, Betty," he said. "I know his life is hid with Christ in God, and you'll see him in heaven. But he really did die in the jungle."

"No, he didn't."

Wendy thought, *The grief has really gotten to her. She's beginning to retreat from reality.* "Betty," he said, "you have to face it: Jim is really dead. He really did die in that jungle."

"No," she said. "Jim didn't die in the jungle. He died when he was a kid in high school. He died when he knelt beside his bed and prayed. He died when he wrote in his journal, 'Gold must be spent. Blood is of no value unless it flows across the altar. Am I expendable? God take me. Spend me any place you need me.' That's when my husband died."

> And what more shall I say? For the time would fail me to tell of Gideon and Barak and Samson and Jephthah, also of David and Samuel and the prophets: who through faith subdued kingdoms, worked righteousness, obtained promises, stopped the mouths of lions, quenched the violence of fire, escaped the edge of the sword, out of weakness were made strong, became valiant in battle, turned to flight the armies of the aliens. Women received their dead raised to life again. Others were tortured, not accepting deliverance, that they might obtain a better resurrection.
>
> Still others had trials of mockings and scourgings, yes, and of chains and imprisonment. They were stoned, they were sawn in two, were tempted, were slain with the sword. They wandered about in sheepskins and goatskins, being destitute, afflicted, tormented—of whom the world was not worthy. They wandered in deserts and mountains, in dens and caves of the earth.
>
> And all these, having obtained a good testimony through faith, did not receive the promise, God having provided something better for us, that they should not be made perfect apart from us.
>
> Therefore we also, since we are surrounded by so great a cloud of witnesses, let us lay aside every weight, and the sin which so easily ensnares us, and let us run with endurance the race that is set before us, looking unto Jesus, the author and finisher of our faith, who for the joy that was set before Him endured the cross, despising the shame, and has sat down at the right hand of the throne of God (Hebrews 11:32–12:2).

Speak to the Aucas about love and they will not understand at all. They did not even have a word for love in their language. But show them men who could have and should have defended themselves and did not, men who were willing to die to bring something to the Aucas, men who counted something more important than even life itself, and they can understand that. Perhaps that's why those same men that killed the young missionaries became the first Christians among the Aucas, finally graduating themselves as Bible college students and missionaries. Precious in the sight of the Lord is the death of His saints.

The Greek word for "witness" is *martyr*. Though indeed we have seen more persons saved in the past century—and especially in the last few decades—than at any other time in history, we have also seen more *die* for Christ in this generation than in any other in history.

The Bible speaks of the last great battle between the forces of light and darkness, between the followers of the Lamb and the followers of the one who poses as the Lion. Against the darkness, heaven will release its warriors, those who hold in their hearts the secret of life over death and the victory of truth over the lie. The conflict will be joined, the battle met, and Satan will be cast out forever, his place found no more. And who will take the final war to him face-to-face and will defeat the devil with the weapons of heaven on earth?

They will know how Jesus won—by laying down His life for the sin of the world. They will have no argument, just the simple record of what happened to them. They will not count their own lives dear. They are heaven's own radical edgers, the holy expendables.

How will Satan lose the last battle? "And they overcame him by the blood of the Lamb and by the word of their testimony, and *they did not love their lives to the death*" (Revelation 12:11).

Leper, are you in?

EPILOGUE

THE MISSIONARY OF THE ONE-WAY TICKET

I will never be the same again.
I can never return I've closed the door.
I will walk the path, I will run the race,
And I will never be the same again.

Fall like fire, soak like rain,
Fall like mighty waters
Again and again.
Sweep away the darkness,
Burn away the chaff,
And let a flame burn
To glorify Your name.

Geoff Bullock
Hill Song Music
From Youth Alive, Australia

MASTER TONIC:
A NATURAL ANTIBIOTIC

IMPORTANT NOTE: As required by law, this information is provided by the right of free speech for educational purposes only, as natural or non-pharmaceutical remedies or therapies are in some nations today often deemed illegal. We must therefore insist that if you are ill or have any disease or health problem that you contact a medical doctor immediately and ask his or her advice before trying any formula, routine or suggestion given in this material.

Whenever I speak on revival and judgement, dozens of people come up afterward and request a copy of this recipe, which is presented during the segment on coming plagues. This is a modern-day version of a recipe for an extremely powerful natural antibiotic originally used to fight infection like the bubonic plague that killed well over a third of the world population in the 1300s. Unlike pharmaceutical antibiotics, this formula fights both bacteria and viruses and is effective against pathogens that have developed immunity to existing drugs.

MASTER TONIC
1 part fresh chopped garlic cloves (anti-bacterial, anti-fungal, anti-viral, anti-parasitical)
1 part fresh chopped white onion, hottest onions available (similar properties of garlic)

1 part fresh grated ginger root (increases circulation to the extremities)
1 part fresh grated horseradish root (increases blood flow to the head)
1 part fresh chopped cayenne peppers (the hottest peppers available, i.e.,
   Habanero, African Bird or Scotch Bonnets, etc.; a great blood stimulant)

Fill a glass jar three-fourths of the way full with equal parts by volume (e.g., a cupful each) of the above peeled, fresh, chopped or grated herbs. Then fill up the rest of the jar to the top with raw unfiltered, unbleached, nondistilled apple cider vinegar. (The solution should look brown and milky.) Close and shake vigorously and then top off the vinegar if necessary. Shake at least once a day for two weeks; then filter the mixture through a clean piece of cotton (an old T-shirt works), bottle and label. Make sure that when you make this tonic that you shake it every time you walk by it, a minimum of once per day. All the herbs and vegetables should be fresh (organically grown if possible), and use dried herbs only in an emergency.

If you find it hard getting any of these particular herbs in your local health food store or grocery store, try asking the produce manager for a special order. If this doesn't work, look for them in an ethnic area of your town. Try markets in Asian, Indian, southern European or South American neighborhoods, where people use these herbs in their everyday cooking. This tonic is extremely powerful, because all the ingredients are fresh. Its power should not be underestimated. This formula is a modern-day plague tonic and when added to an "incurables" routine it can cure the most chronic conditions and stubborn diseases.

It stimulates maximum blood circulation, while putting the best detoxifying herbs into the blood. It strengthens the good guys (probiotics) in your system that help defend against infection that broad-spectrum pharmaceutical antibiotics kill. This formula is not just for the sniffles. It has helped to turn around the deadliest infections like some of the new mutated killer bacteria that defy conventional antibiotics.

The dosage is one-half to one ounce, two or more times daily (one to two tablespoons at a time). Gargle and swallow. (Don't dilute with water.) For ordinary infections, a dropperful taken five to six times a day will deal with most conditions. It can be used during pregnancies, is safe for children (use smaller doses) and as a food is completely nontoxic. Make up plenty; it does not need refrigeration and lasts indefinitely without any special storage conditions.

HERBAL FORMULA FOR IMMUNE SYSTEM STIMULATION
70% echinacea root
10% fresh chopped garlic clove
10% Siberian ginseng root
10% Pau d'Arco inner bark. (Most sold is junk.)

Make a tincture of the above formula with the bare minimum of grain alcohol (Everclear or vodka). For pneumonia and other conditions, use two dropperfuls a minimum of three times daily but six times is better. Use for two weeks, rest a week and use for two more weeks. Rest one month and do it again.

This formula from The University of Natural Healing is Dr. Richard Schultz's adaption of Dr. Christopher's original anti-plague tonic.

Other Books and Resources from LaMar Boschman

The Rebirth of Music

Discover the real meaning and purpose of music.

The Prophetic Song

Understand how the Holy Spirit can sing and play through worshiping believers.

Real Men Worship

Discover how to be a real man who is a real worshiper.

A Passion for His Presence

Discover what the presence of God is and how to live in His presence dailly.

A Heart of Worship

For those looking for worship renewal in their personal life as well as the local church.

Materials available by calling: 1-800-627-0923

For a copy of the Millennium Matrix contact:
Rex Miller at
rexmiller@compuserve.com

Seminars on the subject of this book are available by contacting the author at the address listed below.

Plan now to attend the International Worship Institute. This five-day master worship intensive is held annually in Dallas/Ft Worth, Tx and is attended by hundreds of worship ministers from around the world. Includes over 40 speakers and 120 worshops in all aspects of the worship ministry.

For More Information or a complete catalog contact:
The Worship Institute
PO Box 130
Bedford, Texas 76095
1-800-627-0923
www.worshipinstitute.com

Fill Your Church
With New Life

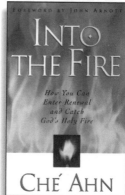
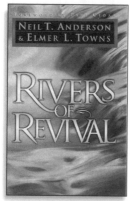

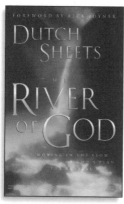

Blessed are the Pure in Heart

Go and Sin No More
Dr. Michael L. Brown
A Call to Holiness

Hardcover
ISBN 08307.23951

What Hollywood Won't Tell You About Sex, Love & Dating
Greg Johnson & Susie Shellenberger
Practical tips to help young people put friendships first.

Paperback • ISBN 08307.16777

Generation Next
Jim Burns
What You Need to Know About Today's Youth

Paperback
ISBN 08307.18095

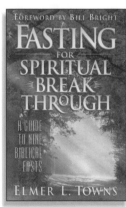

Fasting For Spiritual Breakthrough
Elmer L. Towns
A Guide to Nine Biblical Fasts

Paperback • ISBN 08307.18397
Study Guide
ISBN 08307.18478

Biblical Meditation for Spiritual Breakthrough
Elmer L. Towns
Cultivating a Deeper Relationship with the Lord Through Biblical Meditation

Paperback • ISBN 08307.23609

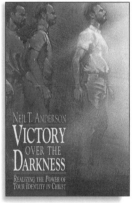

Victory over the Darkness
Neil T. Anderson
Realizing the Power of Your Identity in Christ

Paperback ISBN 08307.13751

Available at your local Christian bookstore.